AS

SIGMUND FREUD

KEY SOCIOLOGISTS

Series Editor: Peter Hamilton
The Open University

KEY SOCIOLOGISTS

Series Editor: PETER HAMILTON
The Open University, Milton Keynes

This series will present concise and readable texts covering the work, life and influence of many of the most important sociologists, and sociologically-relevant thinkers, from the birth of the discipline to the present day. Aimed primarily at the undergraduate, the books will also be useful to pre-university students and others who are interested in the main ideas of sociology's major thinkers.

MARX and Marxism
PETER WORSLEY
Professor of Sociology, University of Manchester

MAX WEBER
FRANK PARKIN
Tutor in Politics and Fellow of Magdalen College, Oxford

EMILE DURKHEIM
KENNETH THOMPSON
Reader in Sociology, Faculty of Social Sciences, The Open University, Milton Keynes

TALCOTT PARSONS
PETER HAMILTON
The Open University, Milton Keynes

SIGMUND FREUD
ROBERT BOCOCK
The Open University, Milton Keynes

THE FRANKFURT SCHOOL
TOM BOTTOMORE
Professor of Sociology, University of Sussex

C. WRIGHT MILLS
JOHN ELDRIGE
Professor of Sociology, The University, Glasgow

GEORG SIMMEL
DAVID FRISBY
Department of Sociology, University of Glasgow

SIGMUND FREUD

ROBERT BOCOCK
Lecturer in Sociology
The Open University, Milton Keynes

ELLIS HORWOOD LIMITED
Publishers · Chichester

TAVISTOCK PUBLICATIONS
London and New York
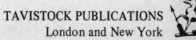

First published in 1983 by
ELLIS HORWOOD LIMITED
Market Cross House, Cooper Street
Chichester, Sussex, PO19 1EB, England

and

TAVISTOCK PUBLICATIONS LIMITED
11 New Fetter Lane, London EC4P 4EE

Published in the USA by
TAVISTOCK PUBLICATIONS
and ELLIS HORWOOD LIMITED
in association with METHUEN INC.
733 Third Avenue, New York, NY 10017

British Library Cataloguing in Publication Data
Bocock, Robert
Sigmund Freud. – (Key sociologists)
1. Freud, Sigmund   2. Sociology
I. Title   II. Series
301'.09214   HM24

Library of Congress Card No. 82-23328

ISBN 0-85312-511-2 (Ellis Horwood Ltd., Publishers – Library Edn.)
ISBN 0-85312-580-5 (Ellis Horwood Ltd., Publishers – Student Edn.)

Typeset in Press Roman by Ellis Horwood Ltd.
Printed in Great Britain by R. J. Acford, Chichester.

Table of Contents

Editor's Foreword   7

Preface and Acknowledgements   11

Chapter 1   Introduction   13
The unconscious before Freud   16
Uses of Freud by social theorists   18
Biographical sketch   26

Chapter 2   Socialization: Language, Gender, Sexuality   32
Sexuality   37
Morality   44
Oedipus   49
Later developments in the study of socialization   57
The Family   59
Gender and Sexuality: (a) Women   60
(b) The Gay Movement   64

Chapter 3   Freud's Social Theory   70
The Death Instincts   71
The Superego   74

Religion and Society   79
Group Psychology   92
The Future of an Illusion (1927)   99
Civilization and its Discontents (1930)   104
Moses and Monotheism (1939)   109

Chapter 4   Methods and Methodology   121
Psychoanalysis as 'science'   121
Sociology and psychoanalysis in the United States   125
Clinical method and psychoanalytic theory   127
Conclusion: Some final reflections   137

Suggestions for Further Reading   140

Index   143

Robert James Bocock is Lecturer in Sociology at the Open University, Milton Keynes, a position he has held since 1979. He was formerly Lecturer in Sociology at Brunel University, London (1966-79): and has, since 1968, additionally lectured in sociology at The Richmond Fellowship College in London. He is a graduate of Brunel University with a Ph.D. in Sociology (1973), and of Leeds University with a B.A. in Sociology and Philosophy (1962).

Dr. Bocock is the author of several articles for the *British Journal of Sociology,* Editor of *An Introduction to Sociology* (1980), and author of two previous books, *Ritual in Industrial Society* (1974) and *Freud and Modern Society* (1976). He has researched and lectured in the USA, Canada, and Tanzania.

Editor's Foreword

The inclusion of a book on Sigmund Freud's theories in a series devoted to *Key Sociologists* may strike some as rather odd, whilst to many it will seem natural and unremarkable. Yet so much of sociology has been created by individuals whose intellectual or social position did not fit in with accepted norms or was in some other ways marginal, that it would be curious indeed to treat Freud as undeserving of sociological attention simply because he founded the science of psychoanalysis rather than that of sociology. He would probably not, of course, have welcomed the title of 'sociologist' but then, neither would Karl Marx have agreed to a definition of his intellectual work as sociology; after all, he even repudiated the label of 'Marxist'! However, no one would seriously deny the centrality of Marx's ideas to sociology just because of his lack of formal involvement with the discipline. It is the ideas themselves and their use by sociology which determines their centrality. Freud, then, is a key sociologist because of his ideas which are so rich in sociological inference and suggestion, because of their consequent appropriation by sociologists of many persuasions, and because the issue of Freud's relevance to sociology has for so long been a focus of intellectual dispute, debate and controversy.

Robert Bocock's study of Freud proceeds from the assumption

that his ideas, concepts and theories have formed vital components of much that is crucial to sociological thought. There can be little doubt, for example, that Freud's ideas about socialization and the family were instrumental in directing much research in this field — sociologists like Talcott Parsons, and social-psychologists such as Erikson, taking Freudian theory as the basis of their own work. Similarly, Freud's theories about the relationship between sexuality and culture have proved to be capable of incorporation within radical sociological theories of ideological domination, and sustained extensive debate about gender and sex roles.

Finally, the clinical concern with psychopathology which forms the cornerstone of Freudian psychoanalysis has similarly found direct application in the sociology of mental illness.

Yet Freud's importance for sociology lies not so much in the direct applicability of his ideas to sociological research, as in the models of society and of social relationships which he developed. His theories constitute a necessary corrective to those 'structural' theories which explain all social action in terms of external processes determined by essentially economic forces. Within such theories questions of the rationality or non-rationality of *individuals* become subordinate to the logic of *systems*. They suffer, in effect, from an inadequacy of description of individual action and behaviour. It would be misleading to give the impression that Freudian theory is the only or best account of individual behaviour; however, its effectiveness in describing rational and (apparently) irrational action has led to extensive use of Freudian ideas to supply models of personality development which are more adequate accounts of social action at the level of small-scale interaction. Perhaps that is why some Marxist scholars (Horkheimer, Habermas, Marcuse, for example) have found Freud a vital complement to Marx in the analysis of repressive domination within capitalism.

As Robert Bocock shows, Freud's ideas have been as easily misapplied as they have been fruitful in developing new fields of enquiry. Unlike Weber, Durkheim and Marx, the theories developed by Freud seem to have been most effective when grafted on to a ready-made theoretical system — to fulfil requirements which otherwise they could not meet. It is arguable whether this has led to an enrichment of those theories or, on the contrary, whether it has led to the masking of a coherent social theory which lies within Freud's work. It is, for example, undeniable that Parsons's application of Freudian theory as a type of 'personality sub-theory' to his 'systems' model seriously distorts Freud. Yet the application leads to plausible and illuminating insights. Similarly, Habermas utilizes Freudian ideas about the development of the analytic relationship as a way of erecting a theory of communicative competence of great utility in understanding repressive ideology. But whether we believe that Freud's own social theory would have generated better sociological models in these or a myriad of other cases, his impact upon sociological thought has been considerable. Robert Bocock is right to ask whether an as yet unknown Freud remains to be discovered, before his status as a key sociologist is universally recognized.

Peter Hamilton

My interest, after making a long détour through the natural sciences, medicine, and psychotherapy, returned to the cultural problems which had fascinated me long before, when I was a youth scarcely old enough for thinking.

— S. Freud [1]

Preface and Acknowledgements

Is Freud relevant for sociologists? Why include Freud in a series about key sociologists? These questions may arise in the minds of some people who pick up this book.

The book aims to show that Freud is relevant to discussions about gender, sexuality, the family, religion, ideology and symbolism, deviance, political authority, socialization and language. This is done by examining some of the ideas Freud developed in his writings which are relevant to this task.

Freud did change his theory over the forty years or more in which he developed it. These changes have not always been given the attention they require in some recent discussions of Freud. In particular his concept of the death instincts has not always been given the role it is given here.

Chapter 1 briefly discusses ideas about the unconscious, or the non-rational in human life, before Freud. Freud belonged to a generation which was trying to incorporate this dimension into a science of man and society. The chapter includes a brief outline of the historical background in which Freud was working between 1895 and 1939.

Chapter 2 examines Freud's theory about socialization and its relevance to the study of the acquisition of gender and sexual orientation.

This chapter contains a brief discussion about the relevance of Freud to recent debates in the Women's Movement and the Gay Movement.

Chapter 3 presents the major social theory to be found in Freud's works. This theory has not always been given the study it deserves by some sociologists and anthropologists. Freud's theory is particularly important in the areas of the sociology of morals, of religion, and of culture more generally.

Finally, Chapter 4 considers the issue of the scientific status, or otherwise, of psychoanalysis. This involves examining the relationship between theory and therapy in psychoanalysis. Therapy was for Freud a method of researching the unconscious. It was not the only method he used in his writings. The methods of sociologists and anthropologists developed and refined since Freud's time are relevant to developing a sociology of the unconscious in societies.

I am especially grateful to Peter Hamilton, Ken Thompson, Alan Waton, Alan Dawe, June Huntington, and the Richmond Fellowship College. They have contributed to my understanding of Freud, especially when being critical.

My special thanks are due to Salvador Giner who read the manuscript and made valuable comments on an earlier draft. Michael Bowman, of Chase Farm Hospital, made comments on some parts of the manuscript too. Neither of them, nor any one mentioned above, is responsible for any errors of interpretation or of argumentation in this book.

Students of the Open University, and on courses at the Richmond Fellowship College, London, have made me aware of the problems involved in approaching Freud, and of the considerable gains to be made when they are overcome. To many of them I am grateful for they have taught me a great deal.

Marie Day has provided great help too, whenever this was possible.

1

Introduction

Freud has had a mixed and uneven reception from sociologists. All sociology courses worthy of the name discuss Marx, Weber and Durkheim — even if the discussion is fairly minimal and the theories and methods developed by these three are later ignored or rejected in the degree programme. With Freud the situation is different. Some sociology courses have ignored Freud's ideas about socialization and about culture and society, while others have given them considerable attention.

One reason for this difference is that Freud is seen as being primarily a psycholgist concerned with the individual, at least in his 'best' work. The more social aspect of Freud's work is often seen as being intellectually weak both by psychologists and Marxists. Sociologists who accept these judgements of Freud will not see any good reason for considering him alongside the major sociologists who founded the subject.

On the other hand there have always been some sociologists, now more than earlier this century, who have not shared these judgements of Freud. Some have taken the view that Freud's work is not only about individuals. For example, the concept of superego in the Freudian schema is one which links well with more sociological views of the way in which we learn and internalise values during socialization. It is not a purely individualistic concept. Freud wrote about the cultural superego too and linked this with his concept of the superego in the individual. There is in Freud, for instance, a theory of religion, its values, beliefs, symbols and rituals which is usually treated seriously by sociologists of religion. This is not to say that the theory is accepted as being true, but that it is not rejected out of hand because it is not a 'proper' sociological theory.

Such views, as will be seen in more detail later, have been developed by Talcott Parsons, a non-Marxist sociologist, and by more Marxist critical theorists such as Herbert Marcuse. The influence of both these major schools of thought, the Parsonian and critical theory developed by the Frankfurt school, have had an influence on many sociologists who now do treat Freud as an important contributor to social theory and to sociology.

More recently, in the last decade or so, there has been a third major influence on the re-assessment of Freud as a major theorist in the social sciences, including sociology, which has come from France. This structuralist approach has fed into debates about gender, culture, and politics in many countries as the texts of Louis Althusser, a French social philosopher, and Jaques Lacan, a French psychoanalyst, have been translated into English and Spanish particularly. Sociologists who have been involved in social and political movements concerned with sexual and gender issues, or with the study of contemporary culture, for example, have taken this work seriously and used it in their writing, research, and teaching.

Psychoanalysis has not been developed within universities, but has established its own organizational framework for the training of analysts and for publishing case material and theory. One consequence of this has been the relative isolation of analysts from other academic disciplines which might be relevant to their work. It has also insulated disciplines such as psychology, sociology, anthropology, philosophy, and literary criticism from informal contacts with psychoanalysts which could otherwise take place within an academic setting.

The reasons for this isolationism come form the academic world, which has typically been suspicious of psychoanalysis, and from psychoanalysts who have maintained a rigid system for training and licensing analysts. Academics have suspected that psychoanalysis is not really a science, but that it is closer to a religion or a theology. One department of theology in the universities has seemed to be quite enough to most social scientists. Psychoanalytic organizational structures have seemed to confirm this view of the religious character of psychoanalysis, in that their doctrines seem to be maintained by the authority structure of the training process rather than by free, open-ended discussion of various propositions which would be found, so it is thought, within a truly scientific discipline. There has been then a mutual complicity in this separation of the academic world from the psychoanalytic world.

Recent developments suggest that there is some loosening of this rigorous separation of psychoanalysis from the academic setting. As has been suggested above there are some courses in sociology, as well as in other disciplines, in which Freudian theory is now discussed. The theory is discussed alongside others which is not at all the same as the way in which analysts are taught the theory for use in their therapeutic work. In the academic setting there are many competing theories, all of which can be discussed openly and assessed for their intellectual merits. In the psychoanalytic setting of training it is assumed by those outside the profession that there is little open-ended discussion of Freudian theory — how could there be when the analysts depend on maintaining the efficacy of the theory and therapeutic practice for their livelihood? However, there has recently been a spawning of therapeutic approaches alongside the one started by Freud and the first schismatic breakaway around Carl Jung. There are now numerous therapies and theoretical schools competing for attention from clients and would-be trainee therapists [2]. The old order of one dominant organization centred on Freud has now completely disappeared.

Within the academic setting, however, it is Freudian theory that is discussed, with little attention paid to other positions. The reasons for this are partly historical and partly intellectual. Historically the major writers who have contributed to the discussion about psychoanalytic theory and various academic disciplines (sociology, anthropology, philosophy, literary criticism) have used Freudian theory. The contemporary discussion takes off from these earlier writers. Intellectually Freud's work is organized in a more rational way then that of others. The later non-Freudian writers tend to concentrate on therapeutic success rather than developing a rationally sustainable theory, and hence their works are of little help to other disciplines such as sociology.

In this book the work of Freud will be discussed in the light of the ways in which various groups of writers have used his ideas within sociology and social theory. This entails selecting from the corpus of works written by Freud those which are most relevant to the later developments within sociology. The aim here will be to outline the major concepts of Freudian theory which are used in many of Freud's papers, books, and case histories, and which are important for understanding later developments in social theory and sociology. The focus is essentially on what might be termed *Freudian social theory* produced both by Freud and by later writers.

This focus upon Freud's social theory is distinct from the way in which Freud is sometimes approached by writers who stress the personality theory in Freud. This is done by both psychologists and by sociologists; it can result in a distorted presentation of Freud's work because the social dimension is overlooked. It is important to focus on the writings of Freud again after many years of discussion about them because various distortions inevitably creep in after different generations of sociologists have taken from them what they need to do for their purposes.

What does Freud's work contain which has attracted the attention of various groups of sociologists? Probably the most important thing is his concept of the *unconscious*.

Although the term was used before Freud, it was he who gave it a special meaning which can be understood only in relation to the theory and practice of psychoanalysis as a whole. Freud took the insights of poets, artists, novelists, and religious mystics into the workings of this aspect of human life and made them into propositions formulated as part of a rational, scientific theory of 'the unconscious'. He was well aware that poets and artists had had the insights he was trying to think about, but they had expressed them aesthetically in works of art, or in religious texts, whereas he aimed to produce a theoretical structure of concepts and propositions which could be used to generate rational, usable knowledge when used in therapeutic practice.

THE UNCONSCIOUS BEFORE FREUD

What were these earlier insights and concerns? They are too numerous to give here, but a few examples may help. 'The child is father to the man' is one such poetic insight which Freud uses indirectly in his theory of the influence of early infant experiences on later adult life.

> Lovers and madmen have such seething brains,
> Such shaping fantasies, that apprehend
> More than cool reason ever comprehends.
> The lunatic, the lover and the poet
> Are of imagination all compact: . . .
>
> Shakespeare (*A Midsummer Night's Dream*, v. 1.2)

And Goethe (1749–1832):

> Man cannot persist long in a conscious state, he must throw himself back into the Unconscious, for his root lives there.
>
> Men are to be viewed as the organs of their century, which operate mainly unconsciously. [3]

There were also some philosophers who developed general statements in the form of a philosophical theory not linked with any methods for relating the theory to concrete, specific, areas, but which nevertheless foreshadow Freud's notion of the unconscious. Schopenhauer (1788-1860) wrote:

> The exposition of the origin of madness ... will become more comprehensible if it is remembered how unwillingly we think of things which powerfully injure our interests, wound our pride or interfere with our wishes; how easily ... we unconsciously break away or sneak off from them again ... In that resistance of the will to allowing what is contrary to it to come under the examination of our intellect lies the place at which madness can break in upon the mind ... [4]

And Nietzsche (1844-1900) wrote:

> "We flatter ourselves that the controlling or highest principle is our consciousness'. And 'All our conscious motives are superficial phenomena: behind them stands the conflicts of our instincts and conditions.' ... 'The great basic activity is unconscious.' ... 'Our consciousness limps along afterward.' ... 'Every extension of knowledge arises from making conscious the unconscious.' [5]

The work of Feuerbach (1804-72), which directly influenced the young Marx, has important parallels with the later work of Freud. This is true of their understanding of religion as based on people's desires and wishes, and whose symbolism is based on dreams. [6] Marx's critique of religion takes off from a similar insight.

Schiller (1759-1805) advised a friend to release his imagination from the restraint of critical reason by employing a flow of free associations.

Vilfredo Pareto (1848-1923), an Italian sociologist whose main work *Trattato di Sociologia Generale* (1916) was translated into English as *The Mind and Society* (1935), developed a view of society as a system of both external and internal forces seeking equilibrium. He was particularly interested in the internal forces which consisted of non-logical residues, as he called them. These were of six main types which included sex residues, sentiments of pity and cruelty among the residues of sociability, beliefs in astrology, the institutions of the family and religion, political ideologies, and a residue of self-preservation. Pareto, like Freud, was influenced by both Nietzsche and Schopenhauer, and their stress on the importance of the non-rational in human societies.

The point of these examples is *not* to show that Freud was less of an original thinker than he is often claimed to be. All original theories can be found in the works of predecessors in one form or another. The point is that there is a sense in which no one knew the insights were there in the earlier writers *before* a thinker like Freud, or Marx, or Darwin, produces a rationally formulated theory applied to specific concrete materials. Once the theory has been so formulated by some-one like these major thinkers then it becomes possible to see the ideas present as insights in earlier writers. They were, indeed, present there, but in an unusable form — in a form which has an emotional effect as in poetry, or as an essay in philosophy, but not in a way which is replic-able, usable by others, and can generate new knowledge in a 'science'.

USES OF FREUD BY SOCIAL THEORISTS

Sigmund Freud founded psychoanalysis, which he claimed was a con-tribution to science. Indeed it was to be a specific science with its own theory and methods of investigation. According to Freud psychoanalysis was to be the only secure foundation for the future development of the social sciences such as anthropology and sociology. Many anthropologists and sociologists have not paid much attention to Freud, although some in both disciplines have taken Freud seriously. Within sociology other major writers have been treated as being more central than Freud — especially Marx, Weber and Durkheim. However, some sociologists have examined and used parts, if not all, of Freud's ideas: first there has been Talcott Parsons, and some influenced by his work; secondly, writers in the Frankfurt School, especially Adorno, Marcuse, and Habermas; finally the French structuralists and post-structuralists, such as Althusser, himself influenced by Lacan, a French psychoanalyst.

These three groups, or schools, of writers sometimes address problems which involve treating sociology as a wide-ranging discipline, with links on the one hand with philosophy, and on the other hand with history and politics. Their use of Sigmund Freud's ideas is differ-ent in each case, but they do all share a concern with using Freud to help them in conceptualizing and understanding the process of social-ization, the entry of the child into human language and culture, and the part played by the irrational in history and politics. These are *central* problems for the discipline of sociology, and are not just luxurious extras.

It is a central problem in sociology to understand the ways in which people acquire the values and ideas which affect their view of society, and of their role in it. This problem has been of importance to

Marxists, for example, concerned with the lack of interest in revolution on the part of many proletarians in West European and North American societies especially from 1914 onwards. Many Marxists had thought it quite possible that the German workers, once in the army, would join with French and British workers in overthrowing the capitalist system which had produced a world war. Hopes were especially high when the Russians had their revolution in October 1917, during the First World War. Looking back, one plausible explanation for the failure of the workers, once armed, to act to produce an overthrow of capitalism, seemed to some to be that they had deeply internalized values and feelings surrounding their respective nationalisms. They found it difficult if not impossible to think of not fighting their country's enemies, so deep were feelings of national identity among ordinary soldiers. This is not to claim that this is the correct explanation – it is being used here to illustrate the reasons why some Marxist sociologists turned to Freudian theory to aid their understanding of the irrational forces in history.

Wilhelm Reich (1897–1957), who was at one stage both a psychoanalyst and a Marxist, became one of the first to try to develop what he termed a sociology of the unconscious, using Freud as he understood him, and Marx, to do so.

This task appeared important to Reich when the Nazis, led by Hitler, won the 1933 German election. The early members of the Frankfurt Institute such as Erich Fromm and Theodor Adorno, also turned to Freudian ideas in order to try to find conceptualizations of the appeal of Nazism which added to, or moved beyond, those of Marxism. This led to an interest in the socialization process, especially in German families in the early part of the twentieth century. The emphasis Freud gave to the role of the father, and to the repression of infant sexuality in the family, led to the development of the notion of the authoritarian personality, by both Reich and Adorno for example. The authoritarian personality was assumed to be a widespread social character type in the German lower middle class; this type of person sought to be led by a strong leader with a clear set of ideas, who put them into action. In some circumstances they too would behave towards others in an authoritarian way – at their place of work, or in the home, towards their children. They would insist that their orders be carried out because they were the authority. When asked for reasons why something should be done authoritarian people tend to reply not with a set of reasons, but with "because I say so, and I'm the boss".

In the United States no such shaking of the foundations of civilization occurred comparable with that produced by Nazism and Fascism in Europe. American sociologists focused their attention on issues such as social control and deviance, as in the work of the Chicago School, and on the processes of socialization, as in the work of G. H. Mead.

These two traditions in American sociology have not used Freud's ideas. On the other hand the giant of American sociology, Talcott Parsons (1902-79) who used the European sociologists, especially Weber, Durkheim and Pareto, but not Marx, did also use Freud.

According to Parsons there are three basic levels of analysis in social science. First there is the level of basic values and symbols, called the culture system. Second there is the system of social roles and social positions called the social system. Thirdly there is the level of the personality system of individual actors in socio-cultural systems. Parsons was concerned with conceptualizing the articulations of the social system with the culture system, and with the personality system. He used Freud's ideas in some detail in his work on the social system and the personality system, and on the way in which cultural symbols are internalized during socialization. He claimed that Freud had made a significant contribution to the theory of internalization of symbols, but that the social system in which socialization was carried out needed to be added to Freud to make it satisfactory to modern sociologists. His work has remained controversial in sociology. Few now claim to be Parsonians, but many sociologists address his work, including Jurgen Habermas, a writer coming from the Frankfurt tradition of critical theory. Habermas has become more eclectic but his work still reflects the influence both of psychoanalysis and Marxism as is typical of critical theorists. His use of the notion of system, and his interest in Parsons, does seem to be at variance with critical theory, however.

Critical theory has always sought to emphasize the need for sociology to stress human agency in history, and this is certainly not emphasized by Parsons. It is, therefore, strange to find Habermas using the notion of system, and the work of Parsons, as he does in *Legitimation Crisis* (1976) [7].

So far the work of the Frankfurt Institute (critical theory) and of Talcott Parsons have been mentioned, and the social and historical locations of their interest in Freud's ideas have been sketched. The work of these later sociologists does affect how Freud is approached now, and some brief understanding of the reasons they became interested in Freudian theory is important in assessing the ways in which Freud has entered sociology.

The work of French structuralists has also been influential in this process of the gradual assimilation of Freud into sociology and social theory more generally. The roots of the structuralist approach, however, are to be found in the existentialism of Sartre which he had developed during and after the Second World War, and in the phenomenology of Merleau Ponty. Sartre had developed a critique of Freudian psycho-analysis, and produced his own existentialist psychoanalysis, which in turn influenced Ronald Laing in Britian. [8] Sartre's critique centred on his extentialist position that there is no Freudian unconscious which can determine, or affect, the free choices of a person as they live their own existence. To Sartre, Freud's concept of the unconscious acting as a determinant, with causal efficacy on people's choices, implied too much of an *essence* in man which could affect his existence. Sartre once defined his extentialism in the aphorism: existence precedes essence. So, in so far as Freud's concept of the unconscious assumed an essence in the psychic life of man, then to that extent it was to be criticized. For Sartre our past cannot affect our choice in the present and future in the way Freud seemed to assume it could.

The origins of this phase of Sartre's existentialism lie in the Nazi/ Fascist period of European history — in his attempt to develop a philosophy which asserted and celebrated man's freedom during the years when men and women fought against modern barbarism. Its failure seemed to many to come in May 1968, when the student-worker revolt against Gaullist France, based to some extent on a philosophy of spontanaeity — a somewhat bowlderized version of existentialism — failed to achieve a change in the regime.

Structuralism was being developed even when Sartre appeared to those outside France to be still the dominant force in French intellec-tual life. Jacques Lacan, the key figure in the structuralist appropriation of Freud, had been developing his ideas during the nineteen-forties. By the early nineteen-sixties his seminars were already key intellectual events in Paris, even before the May events of 1968. After May 1968, however, many who had been involved in political praxis began to turn their attention to psychoanalysis, both as a theory and as a practice.

It was not only in therapy that psychoanalysis became an important practice, but also in the Women's Movement in France and Britain, and in the Gay Movement in France and Italy. Psychoanalysis was turned to as a result of the revived interest in sexual politics. This area has become a central one for the work of linking psychoanalysis, especially that of Freud, with sociology. Both the sociology of the family, of gender and sexuality, and the sociology of deviance, for example, have been involved in recent discussions alongside Freud's psychoanalysis. Although the use of Lacan is increasingly implicit in the recent work, without him Freud would not have become incorporated again into this type of sociology. It is important to point out that although the French Marxist philosopher Louis Althusser has helped bring Lacan, and therefore, Freud, into the centre of some debates in sociology, by no means all those who now refer to Freud because of Lacan are necessarily Althusserians, or Marxists.

The presentation of the ideas of Freud and the assessment made of them in this book is influenced by all three of the schools of thought highlighted above. However, some of the authors already cited have influenced the approach of this book more than others. Perhaps most dominant is the influence of the Frankfurt School, especially Marcuse and Adorno. The work of Habermas has also had an importance. The influences from this group of writers are both epistemological and substantive. Epistemologically critical theory stresses the importance of sociology and social theory being critical of scientism in the realm of methodology. Scientism means here the uncritical attempt to copy the methods of the natural sciences in doing social science. Critical theory tries to retain links between social philosophy and ethics, rather than severing them in order to make sociology appear more like a natural science — something which it is in principle impossible to do anyway as far as this epistemological position is concerned. The social world is *appraised* in the very language used to describe, analyse, explain or understand it. Neutral scientific-sounding language does not avoid such an appraisal, it merely suggests that there is nothing in that which it is analysing to get too worked up about either politically or morally. Critical theory developed its epistemology under the shadow of the Nazi regime, and it has always held that liberal, well-intentioned value-neutrality in the social sciences aided the rise of Nazism by appearing to students and others to be unable to offer any political values worth caring for, thus providing a gap which facism filled.

Substantively, critical theorists have been concerned with the role of the irrational in history and politics, and used Freud to help theorize this concern. For example, in Freud's last major text *Moses and Monotheism* (1939) he seemed to be aware of the possibility of the Final Solution to the problem of the Jews, before anyone outside the Nazi regime knew what had been planned for European Jewry (and one ought to add for gays, gypsies and other misfits too). Critical theorists, such as Marcuse, emphasized the theme of *the return of the repressed* in Freud, and the *social* mechanisms used to enable the collectivities involved to forget, to repress, what has happened in history, so that the repressed returns again. [9]

These macro-historical themes are part of the psychoanalytic theory Freud developed in his work on culture and society. They are a key part of what sociologists can and have learned from Freud. They are also the part of Freud's work many, including some professional psychoanalysts, seem to want to lose. It has been this macro-theory that has been most criticized by anthropologists, philosophers, sociologists, Marxists and non-Marxists. Why? Is it really so poor as academic work? Or does it raise issues which are too emotionally problematic that we want them repressed again, in the name of academic respectability?

The work of Talcott Parsons, and his use of Freud, has had less influence on the way Freud is presented here than critical theory or structuralism. Nevertheless, Parson's intellectual achievement should not be underestimated. He was, and remains, *the* outstanding theorist in recent American sociology. His importance is that he did understand the importance of theory in the development of sociology at a time when pragmatic solutions to particular problems were heavily emphasized.

The work of Lacan (1901-81) and of those writers influenced by him (such as Juliet Mitchell and Guy Hocquenghem) has also influenced this text in important ways. [10] The stress on the importance of language for psychoanalysis, both as a theory and in therapeutic practice, which Lacan made, remains his outstanding contribution. This is in some ways an odd thing to have to say about psychoanalysis because Freud himself did pay careful attention to language in his writings, his interpretations of dreams, and in the speech of analysands. Lacan's work marks the recovery of the *early* Freud, the Freud of dream interpretation, of the Freudian slip (in speech and in writing) and of jokes, witticisms, and plays on words. This parallels the recovery made of the early Marx by some French contemporaries of Lacan during the nineteen-twenties and later. For sociologists and social psychologists the interest in the Lacanian emphasis on language lies in its implications for the way in which children learn to speak and to hear in any language. The learning of language is always said to be central to socialization, and the example of 'feral children' is quoted in many textbooks to illustrate what happens when a child fails to acquire any human language. However, there is a surprising lack of emphasis on the process of learning to speak among ordinary children, or babies, before they go to school, within sociology.

Lacan's conceptualization of the way the individual, or what he terms the subject, is formed as a result of the learning of a language, and of the consequences of this, namely the production of the unconscious in the psychic life of human beings, is of central importance for sociology. Sociologists since Marx and Durkheim have been concerned to conceptualize the processes involved in the production of modern individuals. Freud and Lacan provide essential concepts for furthering the theoretical development of this area. The issues involved here have received a new impetus from the attempts made to understand how human beings become gendered in societies like those of Western capitalism, and how they acquire heterosexual or homosexual orientations to sexual objects, an impetus coming from the Women's Movement and the Gay Movement in these societies.

Lacan also stressed the importance of the scopic drive, and the eye as an organ. Again, since Lacan pointed it out, we can see that this is there in Freud's texts. But until Lacan no one had seen how important this was. For Lacan *the gaze* of the other is the way the baby becomes hooked into socialization at a preverbal level. We each build up a store of images as a result of seeing before hearing and speaking language (called the Imaginary by Lacan) and then normally enter culture through language (the level of the Symbolic in Lacanian terminology).

There is, however, no subject, no real personality at the core of a human being, for Lacan. Here he seems to have retained an important aspect of Sartre's critique of some versions of psychoanalysis, which did assume some central core, a real subject. For Sartre, as for Lacan, there is a lack, a gap, in the inner life of human beings. There is no substantial subject who can be investigated by psychology as though a personality were a thing capable of being measured scientifically. There is action and speech which can be analysed. This cannot be done, however, by objective observations from the outside. To grasp what someone is saying involves some kind of interaction and participation with the other person, as happens in psychoanalytic therapy. The speech of the patient reveals the unconscious, the gap, for Lacan.[11]

The way we read the texts of Freud, and the way in which they are presented here, is affected by these developments. The Lacanian reading of Freud highlights aspects of Freud's conceptualization of socialization processes which were missed, or interpreted in a different way, before Lacan. The critical theorists' reading of Freud, as in Marcuse's reading of Freud's later works, affects the way we now read and present those texts of Freud which discuss phylogenesis (that is the development of the human species in societies) and its links with ontogenesis (the development of the individual in socialization). There are differences in the two epistemological approaches: Lacan is a structuralist; Marcuse and Adorno are critical theorists. It is premature here to try to settle these epistemological differences.

At this juncture it is worth pointing out that Lacan regarded Freud's psychoanalysis as a science, although aware of its 'religious' component.

This is certainly closer to Freud's own understanding of what he was trying to establish than is the position of critical theorists who seek a *rationally* based social theory, incorporating psychoanalysis, but who do not try to develop a social *science* as this is understood by either positivists or by structuralists. Lacan shared some of the disdain for scientism with critical theorists, where 'scientism' means moving from the realm of biology, and animal ethology, to human beings, without acknowledging the great difference it makes that humans possess language, the Symbolic, and therefore the unconscious. Structuralism does not emphasize human agency. Critical theory does emphasize agency, while retaining the understanding of the determinations of social action which were pointed out by both Marx and Freud.

Something must be said about the relationship between clinical practice and the development of psychoanalytic theory, for this crucially affects the relations between sociologists and psychoanalysis. Lacan has been important here for he was a clinical psychoanalyst, but spoke and wrote with little or no reference to his own clinical material. In so far as he reversed the usual relation between the analyst and analysand and asked his patients to talk about Jacques Lacan, it may be he would claim he did use clinical material in his theoretical work! [12] Orthodox analysts insist that psychoanalytic theory can only be developed in conjunction with carefully collected clinical material — one reason for the French psychoanalysts' suspicion of Lacan.

In critical theory, Erich Fromm was an analyst with a clinical practice, but in the opinion of Herbert Marcuse, who did not have a clinical background, this weakened Fromm's capacity to develop critical theory. Clinical practice can mean that the analyst becomes lost in a mass of clinical data, unable to see the theoretical wood for the trees. Reich, who was also a clinician, is now seen by most of his serious critics as poorer in theoretical terms partly as a result of his impatience with careful theoretical work.

Lacan was a clinician who developed psychoanalytic theory independently of his work as an analyst with patients. He is a major example of a clinician who has developed theory in as non-clinical a way as some others who specialized in theory; he did not succumb to the pragmatic, nor to the overly empirical. He also supported the idea of analytic theory being developed in the University of Vincennes by non-analysts. [13] Thus Lacan has an importance in the area of social theory in ways which are unusual for clinicians. These issues will be explored further in Chapter 4. Before moving on to examine Freud's ideas in some detail an outline of the main events in his life follows.

BIOGRAPHICAL SKETCH

It is not necessary to engage in psychoanalysing Sigmund Freud in order to understand the social, cultural and historical context in which he did his work, or the ways in which this social background may have influenced him. That Sigmund Freud's own personality affected the origins and developments of psychoanalysis is a truism. However, the consequences of this truism for assessing the *intellectual* merits of what Freud wrote are irrelevant. Freud's biography is no more, and no less, important to understanding the development and contribution he made to social thought than the biography of any other social scientist is to assessing their contributions. [14]

Sigmund Freud, was born on 6 May 1856, at Freiberg, in Moravia, at that time part of the Austro-Hungarian Empire. The family settled in Vienna in 1860, where Freud went to school. In 1873 he went to the University of Vienna to study medicine. He received his degree in medicine, having specialized in anatomy and physiology, in 1881. Between 1884 and 1887, Freud was interested in the clinical uses of cocaine, and was appointed a Privatdozent (lecturer) at the University, in neuropathology. He went to study in Paris in October 1885, where he studied under Charcot at the Salpetrière, a hospital for nervous diseases.

After Freud returned from Paris in 1886 he did all his important work in developing psychoanalysis, both clinically, and as a more general social theory, in Vienna. The trip to Paris had been important to Freud in shifting his primary concern from academic to clinical research. In particular hypnotism, which involved talking to patients, observing them, interacting with them and not just examining drugged or dead bodies of animals or humans, became important. On returning to Vienna he set up as a private clinical practitioner, specializing in nervous diseases, as he needed more money than he could obtain as researcher in the University if he was to marry and raise a family. He married in 1886, at the age of thirty.

Vienna was a cosmopolitan city, the capital of the Austro-Hungarian Empire until the end of the First World War, and a city whose Jewish population was growing during the last years of the nineteenth century and the first decade or so of the twentieth century. The number of Jews grew from 70,000 in 1873 to 147,000 by the turn of the century. [15] Freud was Jewish by birth, but as an adult was not a participant in the rituals of Judaism, unless there were external reasons for so doing. For example, the fact that only a religious marriage was recognised as a valid marriage by the Austrian State led Freud to marry Martha Bernays in a religious ceremony complementing the civic one. In spite of Vienna's cosmopolitanism there was always a trace of anti-semitism in the city among some of the middle classes long before the Nazi regime institutionalized it (and worse). Freud was always conscious of his Jewish background, and of anti-semitism. His initial support and enthusiasm for Carl Jung, until their break, was that Jung, who was nineteen years younger than Freud and the son of a Christian pastor, was to be the person to take psychoanalysis into the wider world of European culture.

The cultural and social milieu of Vienna during Freud's early years of work has always been the subject of spurious ideas, such as that this environment had produced psychoanalysis because it fitted in so well with the sexual libertarian atmosphere of the city. Freud had himself met this line of thinking in his own lifetime, and had dismissed it in 1914:

> We have all heard of the interesting attempt to explain psycoanalysis as a product of the Vienna milieu. As recently as in 1913 Janet was not ashamed to use this argument, although he himself is no doubt proud of being a Parisian ... The suggestion is that psychoanalysis, and in particular its assertion that the neuroses are traceable to disturbances in sexual life, could only have originated in a town like Vienna – in an atmosphere of sensuality and immorality foreign to other cities – and that it is simply a reflection, a projection into theory, as it were, of these peculiar Viennese conditions. Now I am certainly no local patriot. but this theory about psychoanalysis always seems to me quite exceptionally senseless ... [16]

Freud like many others in Europe, including both Max Weber, and Emile Durkheim, was profoundly affected by the events of the First World War (1914-18). The shift which will be seen later in his theoretical work and which began to emerge in his writings after 1918 was caused, in part, by his attempt to understand how the European War had been possible between civilized countries. Freud was in touch with Albert Einstein about preventing war; they were both concerned with what could be done to stop war happening again. Their attitudes to this problem now seem conventional – education and travel abroad for example – but they did not appear so conventional in the context of the early 1930s when they were written. At that time they were dangerous views to hold.

The Russian Revolution of 1917 had its repercussions on Freud's thinking; he became aware of the attempts made to improve life for millions in that society by economic changes of a fundamental kind. Freud was not a communist, but did admit that he thought a more equal distribution of economic wealth would help improve the lives of many, and might lessen, but certainly not remove, violence and aggression in and between societies. "Aggressiveness was not created by property", he wrote in 1930. He came to think that communism had an incorrect view of human beings. Freud thought that there was a greater capacity in them for cruelty and violence towards others which socialism and communism could just as well feed as prevent or cure.

The attempts made by some psychoanalysts, such as Wilhelm Reich, to link psychoanalysis and Marxism were not supported by Freud himself, who thought that psychoanalysts should aim to be a distinct profession from that of politicians. Psychoanalysis had enough to do in developing its own theory and methods without becoming involved in left-wing political movements; but by the end of Freud's life it became clear that there was nothing analysts could do to prevent others defining their work as subversive, Jewish, and dangerous. Freud and other Jewish analysts became affected by political processes once the Nazis applied their own political philosophy; psychoanalysis did not appear to be a value-neutral science to the Nazis. It was perceived as part of the old liberal democratic, even socialist, Jewish intellectual world. To Stalinist Communists in Russia and elsewhere, psychoanalysis was seen as petit-bourgeois individualism.

More recently Juliet Mitchell has discussed Freud's supposed patriarchial attitudes to women and has tried to rescue Freud's contribution to the theory of socialization into gender roles, especially the role of women, from summary dismissal by some members of the Women's Movement for being too male, phallic dominated. [17] The argument that Freud's theory is invalidated because he held patriarchal values is itself invalid both because Freud was not in fact against women's emancipation, and because such arguments confuse arguments about the validity of a theory with statements about the person, or persons, who developed them. Just as saying that Freud, or Einstein, were Jewish says nothing about the validity of their theoretical work, so asserting that Freud was a male, socialized into mid-nineteenth-century ideas about the roles of men and women, which he never changed, says nothing about the validity or otherwise of his theory about how children are socialized into a gender role and a gender identity.

The end of Freud's working life in the nineteen-thirties took place against the growth of Nazism in Germany, and of Facism elsewhere in Europe. This too played some part in the problems Freud thought about in relation to the social aspects of psychoanalytic theory. This is perhaps especially true of two important texts, namely *Civilisation and its Discontents* (1930) and *Moses and Monotheism* (1939), as well as of many papers written in the nineteen-thirties, and the *New Introductory Lectures in Psychoanalysis* (1932–33).

The problems of human aggression and destructiveness, collective as well as individual self-destructiveness, haunts many of these later writings. Indeed in *Moses and Monotheism* Freud seems to sense that a Final Solution to the problem of the Jews would be found. Freud argued that the problem of the Jews, the self-proclaimed Chosen People of the God of the Christians and of Islam, was not just the same as that of any other non-indigenous group living in Europe. There were, he argued, collective, unconscious, feelings involved to do with Christianity's relationship to the Jewish Father God. The religion of the son in relation to the religion of the primal father – this was the context in which Freud placed anti-semitism.

Collective violence remains the major problem within modern societies, and between them, just as it did in Freud's own lifetime. In his lifetime the violence was on a massive scale in Europe itself. It is partly because Freud was concerned with developing a theory about collective violence from his psychoanalytic work that his writings remain important for sociologists. The work he did in the first two decades of his development of psychoanalysis, mainly between 1900 and 1920, was concerned with socialization and gender, sexuality, guilt and moral values. This work connects with the later material on aggression, in that men are affected by patriarchial exhortations to be good fighters during their socialization.

Freud left Vienna, where he had lived and worked for almost his whole life, apart from visiting the United States, and other cities in Europe, in 1938, after the Nazis moved into the city. He lived for the last sixteen months of his life in London. He had been ill with cancer since 1923, but struggled on with his work. Sigmund Freud died in London on 23 September 1939, at the age of 83.

NOTES AND REFERENCES

[1] S. Freud, Postscript to *An Autobiographical Study* (1925), Postscript added in 1935. Standard Edition, Volume 20, Hogarth Press, London (1959).

[2] See J. Kovel, *A Complete Guide to Therapy. From Psychoanalysis to Behaviour Modification,* Pantheon Books, USA (1976); Pelican Books, Britain (1978).

[3] L. Whyte, *The Unconscious Before Freud,* Basic Books, New York (1960); Social Science Paperbacks, Tavistock Publications, London (1967), p. 128.

[4] Ibid., p. 140. Quotation from Schopenhauer, *The World as Will and Idea.*

[5] Ibid., p. 175.

[6] See L. Feuerbach, *The Essence of Christianity,* translated by G. Eliot, Harper and Row, New York and London (1957).

[7] J. Habermas, *Legitimation Crisis,* translated by T. McCarthy, Heinemann, London (1976). First published in German, 1973.

[8] See J. P. Sartre, *Being and Nothingness,* Methuen, London (1957), especially Part 4, Chapter 2, "Existential Psychoanalysis", and R. D. Laing and D. Cooper, *Reason and Violence. A Decade of Sartre's Philosophy 1950-60,* Tavistock, London (1964).

[9] H. Marcuse, *Eros and Civilization,* Beacon Press, USA (1955); Sphere Books, London (1969).

[10] For a clear discussion of Lacan and France see S. Turkle, *Psychoanalytic Politics Freud's French Revolution,* Basic Books, New York (1978); Burnett Books, London (1982); J. Mitchell, *Psychanalysis and Feminism,* Penguin Books, Harmondsworth (1974); G. Hocquenghem, *Homosexual Desire,* translated by D. Dangoor, Allison & Bushby, London (1978); first published in French in 1972.

[11] J. Lacan, *Four Fundamental Concepts of Psychoanalysis,* translated by A. Sheridan, Penguin Books, Harmondsworth and New York (1979), (French edition 1973). Lacan is not easy to read — but enjoyable when you relax.

[12] See E. Kurzweil, *The Age of Structuralism,* Columbian University Press, New York (1980), chapter on Jacques Lacan. This chapter was reprinted in *Theory and Society:* 'Jacques Lacan: French Freud', Vol. 10, No. 3, May 1981, pp. 419-38. See page 430 of this source for reference to this point mentioned in main text.

[13] See S. Turkle, op cit. (note 10 above), pp. 174-6.

[14] The standard biography and discussion of psychoanalysis remains E. Jones, *Sigmund Freud: Life and Work,* three volumes, Hogarth Press, London, and Basic Books, New York (1953, 1955, 1957). Freud's relationship with Fleiss, and other issues of his biography, are discussed in F. Sulloway, *Freud: Biologist of the Mind*.

[15] See R. Clark, *Freud: The Man and His Cause,* Jonathan Cape, London (1980), p. 84.

[16] S. Freud, *On the History of the Psychoanalytic Movement* (1914), Standard Edition, Volume 14, Hogarth Press, London (1959).

[17] J. Mitchell, op. cit., (note 10 above).

2

Socialization: Language, Gender, Sexuality

The theory developed by Freud can be divided into two broad areas as far as sociologists are concerned. The first of these, to be discussed in this chapter, concerns the processes involved in socialization. One such process is the acquisition of a language by children and another is learning about gender roles and about sexuality generally. The second, to be discussed in the next chapter, concerns the theory of social group life, involving Freud's analysis of authority, moral values, religion, and collective acts of violence. As with any major theoretical position in sociology, each part connects with the whole, and any distinctions of the kind just made are somewhat arbitrary. Clearly, for example, the way in which children learn about sexuality is affected by the religious and moral culture in which they are socialized, and thus there is a major link between the two areas.

Freud himself regarded the concept of the *unconscious* as fundamental to psychoanalysis. It is what makes the psychoanalytic approach distinctive; it is the defining characteristic of the Freudian perspective towards human action. Any new theory in the social sciences must have its own fundamental concepts which found the distinctiveness of the approach which is presented in the theoretical system. Freud used the German term *Das Unbewusste* as the title of a paper written in 1915 which was translated into English as 'The Unconscious'. The meaning of the concept is, however, difficult to define partly because of the changes in Freud's thinking over the years from 1900 to 1939. The term came into the conceptual system from Freud's reflections on the phenomenon of hypnosis as he had seen this demonstrated in Paris by Charcot. It must be possible for the hypnotists' instructions to be retained by a person who has been hypnotized if they later carry out instructions given to them by the hypnotist. They are retained in the unconscious. The work on hysteria Freud had carried out with Breuer in the early 1890s had led him to think that memories of a trauma, experienced in childhood, could have an effect on a young adult, even though the person could not consciously remember the trauma. [1] Here was another phenomenon which suggested to Freud that memories could be retained unconsciously, and continue to have an effect on the adult's life.

Even more significant had been the work Freud did on his own, and on other people's, dreams. *The Interpretation of Dreams* (1900) was a major text in the development of psychoanalysis for it established that dreams could be interpreted and understood if the notion of unconscious dream-work was posited. [2] There is nothing metaphysical implied in this idea; nor are dreams pathological phenomena, but frequent occurrences for everyone.

Until Freud and Jung worked on dreams, educated Europeans had thought of dreams as fairly meaningless. They were seen as leftovers of the day prior to the dream. No great significance was to be attached to them as far as modern, twentieth-century, scientifically minded people were concerned. Other cultures had treated dreams as having a meaning. For example, the Ancient Egyptians in the Bible treated dreams as having a meaning which needed interpretation. Joseph had been able to interpret the dreams of the Pharaoh as containing messages, or predictions, about what was going to happen in the future. In other cultures, dreams of someone who is dead were often interpreted as meaning that the dead were trying to communicate something to the living. Dreams could also be seen as messages from the gods, or spirits.

Freud did two important things for modern European culture. He resuscitated the ancient idea that dreams had meanings, and that the meaning could be discovered by the work of dream interpretation. Secondly, he reversed the way in which dreams had been interpreted in other cultures. Dreams were seen by Freud as having a meaning derived from the *past*, not as having a meaning as predictions about the future. The meaning of a dream was seen as derivable from the past life of the person who had had the dream, and not as a message from a god, or from the spirit world, or from dead ancestors.

The notion of the unconscious became a crucial one for the way Freud found meaning in dreams. The fact that people dream at all was taken as a major example of the activity of the unconscious. Noting the content of dreams gave Freud clues about how processes of the unconscious operated. Many of his axioms about the unconscious stem from the seminal work he did on dream interpretation. For example, the basic proposition that the unconscious is timeless derives from the study of dreams, for in dreams elements from earliest infancy are mixed in with events of the day before the night of the dream in ways which ignore the usual rules we use about time. A second assumption Freud made was that the rules of logic are ignored by the unconscious so that contradictory ideas are placed side by side in dreams. Dreams contain symbols, in which one thing may stand for another, as in the classic example of a tower representing the phallus. This process Freud termed *displacement*. The other main process which gave dreams their character when judged by the rules of normal logic, is called by Freud *condensation*, in which a dream element carries more than one meaning. A woman may be interpreted as being sister, mother, wife (for a man) or a part of the self (for both sexes), when a dream is being deciphered and analysed. [3]

The meaning of symbols in the myths and rituals of religions is in part derived from this work Freud did at the outset of psychoanalysis in *The Interpretation of Dreams*. This needs to be remembered when the Freudian theory of religion is being considered otherwise aspects of that theory can appear to be more arbitrary than they are when set in the context of the methodological assumption that dreams are the royal road to the unconscious.

The same point is true for many other important aspects of the psychoanalytic theory to be considered in relation to socialization. At the time of writing *The Interpretation of Dreams* Freud had not yet developed the theory of the Oedipus stage, but many aspects of this theory are contained in this text on dreams. Likewise the way Freud conceptualized infant sexuality refers back to dreams, as well as to the observations of babies and infants which he made.

As the concept of the unconscious was emerging in the early work of Freud it is important to recognize that many of the ways he used to develop it had nothing to do with patients, or with mental illness. After the work on dreams Freud published *The Psychopathology of Everyday Life* (1901) which examined slips of the tongue, and of the pen (Freudian slips); bungled actions, such as loosing the key to one's house (parapraxes); forgetting words and names; and misreading words. Notice that there is nothing here connected with psychopathology in the sense of mental illness. The focus is on the meaning of common events, which like dreams, no one before Freud had thought of as having any significant meaning. Rather than being seen as having an unconscious meaning such events had been seen as merely accidents, of little importance. Freud seems to deliberately root out for study those areas of everyday life which the general culture of his day defined as having no real significance. His working assumption seemed to be that where events which are fairly common are seen in our culture as of no real significance, there will be found the gap in everyday life which reveals the unconscious.

Having examined dreams, slips of the tongue and pen, the forgetting of names, and parapraxes of everyday life, following this working assumption, Freud turned to wit, jokes and plays on words, such as punning. *Jokes and their Relation to the Unconscious* (1905) examined the ways in which playing with words, and joking, reveal the unconscious. Many elements of the unconscious first make their way into consciousness either by being joked about, or denied. For example, relationships which for some reason are difficult to handle, form the basis of many jokes. The most famous one in this culture is, or used to be, the relation between a young husband and his mother-in-law. There were many jokes about the mother-in-law, and often the mention of 'mother-in-law' in a theatre, is enough to produce a laugh, or at least some nervous giggles.

It is clear now, looking at these early texts of psychoanalysis, that they are concerned with *language and meaning*. Even in dream interpretation, the picture of the dream must first be put into a verbal form before the interpretation can begin. Interpretation involves finding a plausible verbal meaning of the dream — plausible to the interpreter and the dreamer. It now seems obvious that language is so central to the emergence of the field of the unconscious that was to be investigated by Freud and the Freudians, but it has taken the French psychoanalyst Jacques Lacan to bring this out as central. Now Lacan has pointed it out, it is clear that Freud did construct the field of the unconscious in relation to language first of all. [4]

Freud himself did not understand his own work in this way. There is some truth in the criticism made of Freud that he remained embedded in a positivist view of his own work. He thought he had produced a science of the human mind which operated according to the same principles as other sciences — that is that the mind contained flows of energy just as any object in the natural world did. Freud's model of the

way the mind works makes use of a metaphor derived from natural
science, namely that it consists of flows, discharges, and the damming
up of these flows. This model has been called the hydraulic model,
because it suggests water flows as the key metaphor. Others have seen
it as using electricity as its central image from the natural sciences. [5]
In either case Freud did not make it explicit that it is language which is
central to his conceptualization of the mind, and of the way in which
the unconscious is formed.   *pre-verbal psa?*

It is the recent developments in philosophy of language, in linguistics,
and in the study of human communication, and of the social construction of meanings in sociology, which have led many to re-assess Freud's
conceptualization of the unconscious. Language has a central importance
for sociology and psychoanalysis, concerned as they are with understanding and analysing culture, that is symbolic systems, and the
meaning of social action, of myths, and of ideologies.

The Freudian contribution to the study of human language is
unique in that it focuses upon the *imperfections* of human communication, such as forgetting names, slips of the pen or the tongue. It also
focuses on the *surplus* of meaning in human language, as in joking,
punning and double meanings of words. It emphasizes whatever makes
human beings *unlike* computers, unlike technically efficient transmitters
of information. Human beings never speak to one another without
these extra aspects coming into play. Instead of regarding them as
inessential, unfortunate inefficiencies in human communication, psychoanalysis revels in them.

The slippages in human language reveal the unconscious — this is
why they are so intriguing to psychoanalysts who know how to use
them, as Freud did. They do more than just reveal the unconscious;
they show how it was created for a particular person. The words
someone forgets, or misreads, misspells, uses in jokes, slips over when
speaking, or associates with a dream image, are not just accidental;
their meaning lies in the particular unconscious role they play for that
person.

As a baby is reared and socialized he or she is spoken to, and
addressed by others. Slowly each person-to-be is hooked into hearing,
speaking, and sometimes reading a language. At the same time as
learning a language various physiological happenings occur for the baby.
Words become linked with what Freud called instinctual wishes, with
desires. These processes form the unconscious in so far as it is a construct as a result of socialization.

It is important to try to unravel this a little more.

SEXUALITY

The approach taken to the human body by psychoanalysis in theory and therapeutic practice is distinct from a biological, physiological approach. Freud had been a medically trained doctor, interested in the body from the perspective of the biological sciences, but his development of psychoanalysis as a theory and as a therapy marked a major break with this type of approach. This break has not always been understood.

It is important to be clear about this because the theory of psychoanalysis uses the concept of 'instinct' as one of its fundamental terms. The German word Freud used was nearly always 'trieb' which could be translated as 'drive' in English. In a few places in his writings Freud used the German word 'instinkt' when he meant to refer to the biological concept. The Standard Edition of Freud's works uses the English word 'instinct' and so this term has passed into general usage in English discussions in psychoanalytic theory. This convention will be followed here. However, to repeat the point, it must be understood that this word does *not* connote the concept of instinct within the biological sciences. Freud wrote:

> By an 'instinct' is provisionally to be understood the psychical representative of an endosomatic, continuously flowing source of stimulation, as contrasted with a 'stimulus', which is set up by single excitations coming from without. The concept of instincts is thus one of those lying on the frontier between the mental and the physical. The simplest and likeliest assumption as to the nature of instincts would seem to be that in itself an instinct is without quality, and, so far as mental life is concerned, is only to be regarded as a measure of the demand made upon the mind for work. [6]

In another passage Freud made it clear that we can never really know the instinctual wishes directly, for they are always linked with a representative idea. That is to say we never know our instinctual desires without them being mediated by an idea, a word or phrase.

> I am in fact of the opinion that the antithesis of conscious and unconscious is not applicable to instincts. An instinct can never become an object of consciousness — only the idea that represents the instincts can. Even in the unconscious, moreover, an instinct cannot be represented otherwise than by an idea. If the instinct did not attach itself to an idea or manifest itself as an affective state, we could know nothing about it.

When we nevertheless speak of an unconscious instinctual impulse or of a repressed instinctual impulse, the looseness of phraseology is a harmless one. We can only mean an instinctual impulse the ideational representatative of which is unconscious, for nothing else comes into consideration. [7]

In the *Three Essays on the Theory of Sexuality* (1905) Freud develops the first contribution to the psychoanalytic theory of 'instincts'. He draws on material from his patients and from reflections on observations of babies, children and adolescents. (In 1905 Freud decided to publish 'Fragment of an Analysis of a case of Hysteria. (Dora)', although this had been written four years earlier at the end of the therapy. Dora had been 18 years old when she first visited Freud.)

Freud begins these essays by explicitly pointing out that he is introducing a new definition of sexuality from the everyday one.

Popular opinion has quite definite ideas about the nature and characteristics of this sexual instinct. It is generally understood to be absent in childhood, to set in at the time of puberty in connection with the process of coming to maturity and to be revealed in the manifestations of an irresistible attraction exercised by one sex upon the other; while its aim is presumed to be sexual union, or at all events actions leading in that direction. We have every reason to believe, however, that these views give a very false picture of the true situation. If we look into them more closely we shall find that they contain a number of errors, inaccuracies and hasty conclusions. [8]

Freud goes on to distinguish sexual objects and sexual aims. The objects of the sexual wishes may be either a man or a woman for either gender. Men may wish for another male as a sexual object; women may wish for another woman as a sexual object. Sexual objects may be chosen of any age, from the very young to the old. Some people may even choose animals as sexual objects. If this latter idea seems objectionable, the more acceptable form of this – keeping pet dogs, cats, horses, fish, or birds – may seem less so. Sexual *aims* vary from stroking, kissing, looking at or being seen by the sexual object, to genital intercourse, anal intercourse, and sadistic or masochistic practices.

The point of this theory is to break down the notion of sexuality into its component parts in order to be better able to conceptualize and explain the wide variety of human sexual action. Sexual action is action which gives erotic pleasure (even in the form of masochism).

Recent research by sociologists on homosexuality has used the labelling perspective to point out that it is an important issue to know whether the actors themselves apply a particular sexual label to their actions or not. For example, soccer players who hug and kiss one another after some player has scored a goal may not label that action 'homosexual' or 'gay' in the way some observers might do. Does this mean that no one can say whether the action of the footballers is really homosexual or not? Clearly it depends upon who answers the question. This would seem to imply that there is no way for sociologists, or anyone else for that matter, to fix a label or a meaning to any particular action. This perspective often leads sociologists to deny the validity of the labels psychoanalysts use.

This type of argument leads to the conclusion that no explanatory theory at all is possible in the social sciences. On this view sociologists should produce ethnographic reports of different groups and in this way relativize all absolutist religious, political or social scientific positions. Sociological reports would show that in fact a multiplicity of ways of construing the world, including sexuality, exists. No one of these ways is intrinsically any better than any other. In so far as psychoanalysts report the life histories of individuals as they themselves experience their lives, then they can be seen as making a valid contribution to the knowledge we have of others. The clinical case history, shorn of theory, is the way forward on this view, rather than developing the theoretical speculations of Freud.

Such a position rejects Marx and Marxism as well as Freudian theory. It also rejects Parsonian sociology. This needs to be borne in in mind in this context so that Freudian theory is not seen as the only target of this kind of sociological relativism.

The labelling perspective has been very useful in making people aware of what they are doing when they apply a particular label such as 'homosexual' or 'invert' to someone. Psychoanalysts certainly need to be reminded of the dangers involved in applying their concepts, turning people into cases, and thereby fixing them in categories. Equally sociologists who use the labelling perspective in its purist form need reminding that their position of complete relativism is unnecessarily restrictive. Sociologists and social theorists are entitled to develop their view of the social world according to what they see as rational explanatory principles. Indeed there is nothing the labelling approach can say, while remaining consistent with its own principles, to those who persist in developing categories and labels for others. All that can be done is to show that others do it differently, to which adherents of absolutist positions may say, 'So what?'

Freud developed a new discourse, a new conceptual language and an explanatory theory, for a range of phenomena he delineated by the term 'the unconscious'. Central to the theory which tried to explain dream symbolism and the symptoms of some of his clients was the specific psychoanalytic concept of sexuality. This conceptualization broke sexuality down into a number of constituent components. These were called *component instincts.* [9] They varied according to their aim, their object, or their source. We have already discussed aims and objects briefly. The sources of an instinct can be either an orifice or a process of the body. Infants derive pleasure from the mouth through imbibing milk. They may derive pleasure from the anus by the holding back and letting go of their faeces. They may derive pleasure from touching their penis or clitoris, from being fondled there by adults or other children. They may enjoy showing their genitals, or seeing others. They may equally find pleasure in urinating and in watching others of the same or other sex urinating or defecating.

The concept of sexuality within psychoanalysis has a quite specific meaning from that in ordinary common usage. Ordinarily people use the word sexuality as synonomous with adult heterosexuality. In Freud's psychoanalysis the word refers to the concept of polymorphous sexuality, and includes infant sexuality as well as that of puberty and adulthood, homosexuality as well as heterosexuality. The concept of polymorphous sexuality means all the variations of sexual objects, aims and sources Freud discussed in the *Three Essays on the Theory of Sexuality* that were briefly outlined above. This is, therefore, a much expanded notion of sexuality from that of ordinary language. The variations found in sexuality are known within psychoanalysis as the component instincts of the general category 'sexual instincts'. These variations include oral, anal, phallic, and genital, sources of sexuality; variations in aim such as voyeurism, exhibitionism, sadism, masochism, and oral, anal, or genital intercourse; and finally variations in objects from opposite gender, same gender, younger, or older people, to animals, fetishized objects, and coprophilia. These variations may be seen as perversions in particular cultures, but they are assumed to be fairly universal components of even adult genital sexuality. Freud wrote: 'No healthy person, it appears, can fail to make some addition that might be called perverse to the normal sexual aim; and the universality of this finding is in itself enough to show how inappropriate it is to use the word perversion as a term of reproach'. [10]

For Freud the theoretical importance of the sexual instincts could not be overestimated within psychoanalysis, even though others, starting in 1912 with Carl Jung, have sought to lessen the importance which Freud gave to his ideas of sexuality. This theoretical importance was based on Freud's therapeutic work with his patients, who were at this period of his career (1896–1918) mainly people from 18 to 40 years of age, many appear to have been with hysterical symptoms, and with high anxiety. Jung came to focus on young schizophrenics and upon quite successful people in various professions who were over 35 years, and this therapeutic practice led him to stress the individual's inner world, and sense of meaning and purpose in life. Freud emphasized relationships between people more than Jung. Jung concentrated on the internal process of 'individuation', and although superficially his concept of the collective unconscious would appear to link directly with sociology, it is Freud's work which has turned out to be more useful in linking psychoanalysis and sociology.

It is important to recognize that Freud's own theory did undergo changes especially after 1920 when he made some important additions to his conceptualization of the instinct theory. He always retained the early emphasis on sexuality, however, from the *Studies of Hysteria*, written with Joseph Breuer, and published in 1895, through to his final works.

The psychoanalytic contribution to the understanding of socialization is, therefore, very much concerned with the relation between infant sexuality, and the introduction of the child into human culture and society by learning a language in a family setting of some kind. The psychoanalytic stress on the baby's *body*, on fundamental bodily pleasures such as being held, stroked, and fed, and later on toilet training, is an important emphasis to avoid 'the over-socialized conception of man' — a term introduced by Dennis Wrong in his critique of some sociological theories of socialization. [11]

Without some notion of the body, theories of socialization have been liable to develop a view of the human infant as a completely empty vessel into which anything may be poured. The adult is seen as a product of a particular culture, or sub-culture, who has made no contribution to their own development and ideas. The deviant young person or adult is then seen as someone who has been under-socialized and who is consequently in need of more socialization in a training centre of some kind. The psychoanalytic perspective does draw attention to the contribution that the young person, infant, baby or child, makes to their own socialization. This perspective moves beyond focusing on the processes which have been called 'internalization of cultural symbols' (by Talcott Parsons, for example). Even babies are not only internalizing cultural values and other symbols, but also they are *rejecting* some attempts to have them behave in particular ways. They may also be actively striving to *create* their own satisfactions from a very early age. Babies, infants, children, and young people are seen to be not only passive recipients of a process of induction into a human culture, but also actively engaged in a process of creating a pleasurable situation for themselves too. This active engagement in creative play is derived from the component instincts of infant sexuality in Freud's theory — from bodily wishes and desires.

There is still a problem about how social scientists, including psychoanalysts and sociologists, can know what these bodily wishes and desires are. If they are always presented to the unconscious and to consciousness in verbal form, as Freud suggested in the passage quoted earlier, then there are difficulties in saying what they are prior to the baby learning a language. However, Freud seems to have been able to establish something about the content of these instinctual wishes from three main sources. First, he observed the physical symptoms of his patients, such as persistent coughing, vomiting, or pains in the neck, fainting, dizziness, stammering, or gastric pains. These symptoms were interpreted by Freud as having a meaning which could potentially be turned into words — not just by the analyst but importantly by the patient. The underlying meaning of these symptoms he claimed he found was sexual. The symptom could be seen as a way of communicating a wish, or desire, which could not be expressed in either words or in deeds. A form of censoring was operating in the young people Freud saw — they had learned that some of their desires were 'bad'. Nevertheless the desires were still there exerting a persistent pressure which sought an outlet in some form. Therapy could cure some hysterias if the patient could verbalize the desires to the analyst. [12]

Secondly, Freud had gained much valuable information from the analysis of dreams. The weird images in some dreams began to make sense if they were interpreted as having a meaning, albeit in a disguised, or symbolic, form. Again Freud found the process of censorship operating in the way dreams were constructed by 'dream-work'. Very often there was an unexpressed erotic wish lying behind a symbol in a dream. Sometimes the wish might be fulfilled in the dream images themselves, and may or may not be described in the dreamer's verbal report of their dreams. Here a form of conscious or unconscious censoring is operating again Freud assumes. The censoring leads to the non-expression of the desire in the first place. The desire is expressed neither verbally nor in action by the dreamer. But the desire persists in the unconscious to become the stuff dreams are made of.

Some dreams show the action of censorship in the unconscious while the dreamer is asleep, Freud claims, because without some such assumption as this dream symbols do not make 'sense'. With such an assumption Freud found he could interpret many strange dream symbols. It is here that notions like that of phallic symbol belong in the corpus of psychoanalytic theory. For example, some one may dream of towers, or tall buildings, or aeroplanes and these elements in a dream make sense to the patient when seen as linked with desires for a phallus — perhaps of some young man the dreamer saw the day before or many years ago in their infancy (their father). Such desires may lie hidden in the dreams of women, young and old, and of men of any age too. The desire may be for some form of bodily contact with the phallus expressed in disguised form in a dream.

Thirdly, Freud made unsystematic observations of infants and children. He used these observations to develop his understanding of infant sexuality and desires. He also made use of reported conversations with children, as in the case history of the five-year-old boy known as Little Hans, whose father recorded his conversations with his son and gave these written reports to Freud. Out of this kind of material Freud developed further his ideas about infant sexuality. It acted as a check on the reports his patients gave him of their own childhood acts and wishes. [13]

Freud noticed that children as well as psychoanalysts like himself had theories of sexuality. Some children thought that fertilization occurs through the mouth and birth through the anus; that parental intercourse was sadistic, and that both sexes possessed a penis. These views were held by children of different ages before puberty, and they are mainly but not entirely derived from small boys. They are also derived from children brought up in the last decade of the nineteenth and first decade of the twentieth century who were normally being told that babies were brought by the stork. Children did not believe this, and so invented their own theories. Freud does recommend that children should be told how babies are produced by teachers or by their parents, as some children now are in Western societies in the last few decades of the twentieth century. He does say that at 10 or 11 years of age children may be told by other children who do know the true facts of intercourse and birth, but that they cannot understand fully because they are still ignorant of semen. Earlier in life they are ignorant of the vagina — this presumably applies to girls as well as boys. It is unclear how far parents telling young children could actually communicate a reality based understanding to their children about sexual intercourse and childbirth. Freud would seem to be suggesting that young children will reject or distort such information. This may be — it is very little researched by sociologists or psychoanalysts so we do not know what children are being told, by whom and when in modern societies on these matters. However, the secrecy about sexual knowledge could well be altered by progressive education and in families, where adults discuss where babies come from with their young children. [14]

The Freudian theory of sexuality has an importance for sociologists because it provides a way of conceptualizing the relations between the human body, and its wide variety of potential sources of erotic pleasure, and socialization into a human culture. Freud's theory is a mixture of general theoretical propositions, and ideas about socialization in a particular culture — namely German middle class and peasant families in Austria at the end of the nineteenth, and the beginning of the twentieth, century. It is also written at times primarily from the point of view of boys, but includes ideas generated in therapeutic work with young women too. These particular aspects of the theory need to be distinguished from the more universal general theory of sexuality and socialization in a way which Freud himself failed to do.

It is important to notice that the two types of proposition coexist in the first formulations of the theory, but that to point this out is not to say anything about the usefulness, or truth or falsity, of either the account of socialization into German culture or of the more general theory. So it is not very helpful to simply point out that Freud's theory is written by a man who worked in Vienna with middle class Viennese patients brought up in the 1890s or the 1900s. This sort of statement fails to point out that there is a more general theory involved. It consequently fails to discuss this latter theory.

From the above presentation and discussion of the Freudian theory of infant sexuality two major points should be noticed for later discussion. The first is that Freud is positing that there is a wide but specific range of erotic desires in human bodies at birth. These are unknowable to the individual except through verbal ideas to which they are attached in infancy, although psychoanalysis is able to build up some knowledge about them from dream interpretation, therapeutic work, and observations of what children do and say. The second point is that infants are introduced into a human culture, and a language, within a family, and that this affects the particular constellation of desires in particular individuals. This process does not fully mould or create these desires. Indeed the process of socialization is affected by the instinctual wishes of children, as well as affecting these same wishes through censoring some of them.

MORALITY

At the same time as Freud was working on his theory of infant sexuality within the framework of psychoanalysis he was thinking and writing about more specifically sociological matters. In 1908 he published a paper on *'Civilized' Sexual Morality and Modern Nervous Illness'*, [15] in which he distinguished three types of sexual moral systems in different societies and traced their effects on those socialized into them. The three types of morality were:

(1) A moral system in which sexual instincts 'may be freely exercised without regard to reproduction'. There is not an absence of morality in such a situation. People are expected to conduct themselves in ways which respect others. They may enjoy sexuality with others just for the enjoyment of the activity, with either same or opposite sex partners.

(2) A moral system which suppresses sexuality except that which serves the aims of reproduction. This may be with a number of partners inside or outside marriage.

(3) A moral system which is 'civilized' in the sense used in this context by Freud. Only sexual acts which aim directly at reproduction with one and the same partner throughout life are regarded as morally good. All other sexual acts are in varying degrees less moral, or just plain evil, doings.

Freud thought that in the period in which he was writing in Vienna the second type of morality was the most widespread, but with both orthodox Jewish and Roman Catholic religious authorities upholding the third type of morality. Since Freud's time Western societies have changed to some extent so that they now contain all three types of moral system. There is an uneasy acceptance in some Western societies that sexual pleasure may be pursued by both heterosexuals and homosexuals. Most public figures uphold the second type of morality, and the Roman Catholic Church and its followers uphold the third type of moral system.

Freud was concerned to show the effects of these moral systems on different groups of people. In doing so he made certain assumptions. One such assumption was that people are born with a certain strength to sublimate their sexual instincts which varies from one person to another. Some people are more able than others to repress their sexuality and to direct their more perverse sexual desires into culturally valued activities, such as scientific or artistic work. This process Freud called *sublimation*. Education aims at directing the young to sublimate their sexual desires into a variety of socially acceptable and useful activities from mathematics, to art, to sport.

Another assumption Freud made was based on his therapeutic work. This was that the strength of sexual drives in some people could be so strong that they could not sublimate all or most of their sexuality into such socially useful actions. Such people either acted on their strong sexual instinctual drives, and managed to handle the actual or potential disapproval of society's moral guardians, or they succumbed to illness, especially psychoneuroses. The first group, the perverts, the homosexuals and lesbians, Freud saw as stronger in that they could reject the attempts made by religious, educational, legal, and familial authorities to make them conform to a morality they found impossible to live by.

Those who were weaker conformed outwardly to the moral system, but this conformity was won at a great cost to them. Although weak in this respect these people often had some sexual drives which were very strong. These sexual energies were not capable of cultural sublimation, either because they were too strong for that, or because the person lacked any special intellectual or artistic skills, or they were never developed in them. This second group were those who fell ill with psychoneurotic disturbances for this was the only way in which the sexual drives could obtain satisfaction, or at least some indirect draining off of their energies.

Given that there has been some controversy about Freud on women, it is worth noting that at this stage in his work he was very aware that women had fewer opportunities in education, in occupations, and were more involved in rearing families than men. This led to more women than men being subject to psychoneurotic illness because they had less opportunity than men to sublimate their perverse sexual desires through education and professional work. Equally they had fewer opportunities outside the home to act on their perverse sexual desires than did men. Freud wrote: 'in many families the men are healthy, but from a social point of view immoral to an undesirable degree, while the women are high-minded and over-refined, but severely neurotic'. [16]

In the same paper Freud also assumes that women have less strong sexual drives than men just because they are women. 'Quite frequently a brother is a sexual pervert, while his sister, who, being a woman, possesses a weaker sexual instinct, is a neurotic whose symptoms express the same inclinations as the perversions of her sexually more active brother'. [17] No more details are given of quite what Freud had in mind here! However, there is in such passages, a rigid view of the differences between the sexes which seems to derive from an assumption that such differences are determined biologically. At other times Freud makes it explicit that he assumes there is a high degree of constitutional bisexuality in both sexes, although the balance between heterosexual and homosexual desires varies from one person to another.

The situation is further complicated by the fact that psychoanalysis cannot establish what is constitutionally determined, for this would be the task of a different science, such as genetics. Psychoanalysis is concerned with the interaction between the potentialities in the body for a variety of erotic pleasures and the process of socialization. The best assumption to make is that until proved otherwise all differences between people, and between men and women, are a result of socialization interacting with body. All human bodies should be assumed to have the same potentialities for erotic pleasure within the disciplines associated with psychoanalysis and sociology. This does not mean that constitutional, or genetic, factors and variations between people should be assumed to be non-existent, but that within social science we do not know them. Freud's theory does allow for such constitutional factors, but at times he assumes he knows more about them than is possible within psychoanalysis.

In the oral and anal phases, up to two or three years of age, children experience similar pleasures and pain whether they are boys or girls. Both boys and girls have similar pleasures and pains in relation to the breast and in relation to being washed, dried, urinating and defecating. They both have their first experience of social control in the anal phase in relation to being toilet trained. In 1920 Freud added a note to the *Three Essays on the Theory of Sexuality*:

> Lou Andreas-Salome (1916), in a paper which has given us a very much deeper understanding of the significance of anal erotism, has shown how the history of the first prohibition which a child comes across — the prohibition against getting pleasure from anal activity and its products — has a decisive effect on his whole development. This must be the first occasion on which the infant has a glimpse of an environment hostile to his instinctual impulses, on which he learns to separate his own entity from this alien one and on which he carries out the first 'repression' of his possibilities for pleasure. From that time on, what is 'anal' remains the symbol of everything that is to be repudiated and excluded from life. The clearcut distinction between anal and genital processes which is later insisted upon is contradicted by the close anatomical and functional analogies and relations which hold between them.[18]

During the next phase of psychosexual development, the phallic,

Freud assumed that at the start both boys and girls are interested in the penis and that girls enjoy erotic pleasure from their clitoris. Girls want to see a boy's penis, and sometimes try to urinate from the same sort of position as boys. They and their brothers assume, according to Freud, that the little girl will grow one soon when they compare their bodies. The phrase 'penis envy', which has caused so much misunderstanding, is used initially to describe this fascination with the penis by both sexes in this early part of the phallic phase. The assumptions Freud made could be empirically mistaken, or could be true of his time and place but not universally true. Neither he nor his later critics have really done full studies to discover what is going on between boys and girls around the ages of two and three. This lack of research is because the issue is linked with psychoanalytic theory and psychoanalysts change their theories on the basis of clinical evidence derived from work with patients and not by conducting systematically sampled observations from a variety of cultures and classes, as sociologists would do.

A further point may help clarify Freud's position at this juncture. This is that the penis in the phallic phase is assumed to be the only sexual organ there is — Freud asserts that boys, and girls are ignorant of the vagina, and that they assume that their mother has a penis too for she is a grown up. At this stage Freud is saying that children do not distinguish the two genders, male and female, in the way they will after the Oedipus stage, in the later part of the phallic phase. The penis for children of this stage is *not* the genital organ of the post-pubertal male, capable of ejaculation of semen. It is the part of the body which seems to give pleasure when touched, as does the clitoris for the girl. It is in the phallic phase that both boys and girls experience for the first time erotic pleasure linked with the part of the body that will later on be the centre of their adult, genital sexual lives. In the oral and anal phases pleasure is gained from the orifices connected with the intake and expelling of foods and liquids. These pleasures are the base of the erotic forepleasures of adult genital sexuality, and for adult perverse sexual actions. The phallic phase is the basis upon which genital sexuality is built after puberty in boys and girls. For children, ignorant of the adult males' semen and of the adult woman's vagina, the little penis signifies their first encounter with sexual differences — possession of a penis or not.

Freud's account seems strongest when he is distinguishing between phallic stage conceptions of the penis and genital conceptions of the penis, when, after puberty, it can ejaculate semen. His account is weakest when he assumes an ignorance of the vagina on the part of boys and girls. Young children do try to play at 'mummies and daddies' and boys sometimes lie on top of girls trying to place their penis on, or even in, the hole in the girl. (Children used the English word 'hole' as a slang word for the vagina.) If Freud had said children were ignorant of the role of the womb, and the female egg, this would be more akin to the ignorance of semen, and would be much more plausible. The assumption of ignorance of the vagina in the phallic phase appears to be the weak point in the theory so far.

OEDIPUS

Children come to be introduced to the wider society and culture during the later half of the anal phase, and they begin to learn to hear language and to speak themselves. In spite of the fact that Freud did emphasize the role of talk in the therapeutic situation, he did not highlight the process of learning to hear and speak a language by the child. Since the end of the Second World War the role of language has moved into the centre of attention, both in philosophy and some sociological uses of psychoanalysis, although with a few exceptions most sociologists have not so far paid much attention to it.

In Freud's theory the introduction of the child to society and culture becomes more important during the later part of the phallic phase — during the Oedipus phase. It is in this phase that the child begins to learn how to act as a good little boy or little girl as these roles are defined in the culture, or sub-culture, into which they have been born. There are two aspects involved here: learning what it is to be a male or a female in a particular cultural group, and learning what is seen as good and bad action in that group as represented by the child's parents, and especially, in this culture, by the father.

The ideas surrounding the concept of the Oedipus phase, or complex of feelings, had been around in Freud's thinking from very early on in his work. Sophocles' play *Oedipus Rex* is discussed in *The Interpretation of Dreams* (1900).[19] In this text Freud also mentions Shakespeare's *Hamlet* as a play rooted in the same soil as the ancient Greek play, but under more disguise. In the play by Sophocles, Oedipus kills his father, King Laius, although Oedipus does not know it is his father whom he has killed. He had been sent away from his father's house because of the King's fears of his son based on the oracle's predictions of the parricide. Oedipus, unknowingly at first, marries his mother, Jocasta. When he discovers what he has done he blinds himself. This play deals with the emotions all children handle in the late phallic phase, Freud claims.

It is important to remember here the assumption of unconscious bisexuality as being a fundamental part of psychoanalytic theory. A small boy is experiencing feelings of love and attraction towards his mother in the late phallic phase. He also experiences feelings of intense hostility towards any male who is his rival for his mother's affections. In this society, until the recent development of single-parent families, the male who is the boy's erotic rival is also the one who is used as a final form of social control. 'I'll tell your father about it' was a phrase used as a way mothers tried to control children, and still is in some families. The 'masculine' part of the girl is experiencing the same feelings as the boy − and here it is important to remember that baby girls have the mother as their first object of attachment. The other, who is usually the father, the man in mother's life, but could be another lover who is not the biological father of the child, is a rival to the mother–child bond as the child comes to perceive the other in mother's life.

Oedipus is approached from the point of view of the son, and from the point of view of the part of the daughter's unconscious which loves the mother. This is not an example of Freud's patriarchal male bias. Rather it is approached in this way because this is how children approach the Oedipus phase themselves − from mother as their first love object. Girls as well as boys approach the external world from this bond with mother.

To say this is not to say that it must be like this as a fact of nature. It is possible to conceive of a culture, or even of already existing sub-cultural patterns, in which the primary care of the new-born baby is carried out by a male, not by the baby's biological mother. Such a situation may alter the child's feelings towards its biological mother, and towards its father, and these changes may have effects on the child's choice of man or woman as a sexual and love partner in later life. However, such changes would not alter the first experience of another person as a primary figure for affection, and of the feeling of hostility towards the other person who comes in to interfere with this bond between the child and its primary care figure. Nor would two such primary care figures avoid the issue − some of Freud's patients had been brought up by nursemaids as well as having a person defined to them as social and biological mother. Such arrangements for child-care do not avoid the entry into the world of other people who are not carers for the child, yet it is this disturbance in the infant's world of being cared for, of being fondled and loved, which sets up the feelings of hostility towards some other person first of all.

There is another side to the issue in any case, quite apart from the issue of who, or of how many, do the primary care work of the baby. This is that just as girls have a masculine part which has related to their mothers, so boys have a feminine part of their unconscious which takes an attitude of love towards father, or the male figure who is close to them during this phase of socialization. Girls have a feminine part in their unconscious which also seeks love from father, or the male figure in their lives at this time.

Freud rejected the use of the term Electra complex, introduced by Jung, for these feelings of love towards the father and hatred towards the mother figure by the feminine part of both sons and daughters. [20] Freud thought that the notion of the 'feminine Oedipus complex' was sufficient. The term 'Electra complex' would not be the correct one to use in any case in this context, if the intention was to draw on the oldest of the Greek myths and plays. It is worth following this up further in this context because doing so will point up a theme which is not developed by Freud, but has been important in psychoanalytic developments since he died.

Electra was the daughter of King Agamemnon and his wife, Clytemnestra. She had a brother, Orestes. In the triology by Aeschylus, *The Orestia*, first performed in 458 BC, and based on Homer's *Iliad* and *Odyssey*, it is the son Orestes who kills his mother, not Electra. It is true that Electra hates her mother and wants her killed by Orestes in the play and myth. The children want their mother killed because she had killed their father, Agamemnon, and had installed his cousin, Aegisthus, as her lover and as King. So the ancient Greek term to describe the converse of the Oedipus complex of feelings would be the Orestes complex. This would point up the feminine side of the son, and the feminine part of the daughter, and the feelings of hatred for the mother and of some affection for the father.

The resolution of the conflict of feelings experienced by children in this stage of their development takes different forms for boys and girls, at least in this culture with its different conceptions of the gender roles for men and women. The writings by Freud on this are again a mixture of propositions about a general process of the introduction into human society and culture for any human beings, and an analysis of how this process is achieved in a particular culture in the first three decades of the twentieth century. This does not make it easy to know which propositions are which. Freud had no such distinction in mind when he wrote so there are few if any signs from him as to which propositions he thinks of as being general, and which are particular to one cultural situation.

Freud writes in his later works, especially in the paper 'Female

Sexuality' (1931)[21], that the pre-Oedipal phase is important for girls particularly, in that their relationship with their mother figures varies in its length and in its intensity. In one sense girls find it easier to make the appropriate identification with their gender than do boys, for they have a continuity between the affection they feel for their mother and the adult role of being a woman. Boys, on the other hand, have to move from their affection for their mother and hostility to their father, towards a positive identification with their father and so to act in ways appropriate to males. Boys have to make a jump from early positive relationships with women and hostile feelings to men across to positive identifications with men. Freud thought that one consequence of this change was a permanent disparagement of women by boys and men after they make this jump. This is not a justification of such disparagement, but it is an analysis of it.

To return to the resolution of the Oedipal conflicts for the boy. The boy makes the transition from hatred of the father figure to identification as a result of the threats of castration made to him by men and women. He is told that he must not play with his own penis, that he must not masturbate in his infantile manner, and that if he does he will lose it. His father, or the doctor, will come and cut it off. Boys who have seen little girls know this is a possibility. Girls are not now people whose penises have not grown; they are people like himself who have had them cut off.[22] For the boys at this stage there is no real distinction between having his penis cut off and having his testes removed. 'Being castrated' to an adult male means to have testes cut off. To the small boy it means having his penis cut off — in any case his testes are unimportant to him psychologically, and will be until puberty.

To avoid castration, which is a real threat, especially for those boys who have seen girls without a penis, it is best to make peace with the father who threatens castration. Boys typically come to identify with their fathers as those who have power and authority, that is the power to cut off his penis. This begins the development of what Freud came to call the superego, in *The Ego and the Id* (1923). The superego performs the role of the censor as Freud had termed this aspect of the psyche up to the introduction of the id, ego, superego model.

This identification with the father dissolves the Oedipus complex for the boy who becomes the typical, normal, male in this type of society. The conflict of feelings is completely dissolved, and not repressed into the unconscious as it is with those boys who do not make a successful enough identification with their fathers, or other male figures. For example, some boys resolve Oedipal feelings by identifying with their mothers with whom they have had a strong and lasting relationship since being born. Such boys are likely to be homosexuals when they are adult, seeking to love boys through their identification with their mother who loved them. This is not the only reason for homosexuality. Boys with a strong predisposition towards feminine passive behaviour towards their fathers and other males are likely to resolve Oedipal conflicts this way according to Freud.

The resolution of Oedipus by girls in this society is discussed by Freud as being more different from that of boys than he had at first thought. The main reason for this change was the discovery of the key importance of the pre-Oedipal stages, especially the relationship with mother. Freud likened this discovery of the pre-Oedipal level to that of the discovery of the Minoan–Mycenaen civilization behind the civilization of ancient Greece in archaeology. It was a fundamental layer without which the later developments could not take place — the individual and the group could not reach a level of 'civilization' without it.

In the paper 'Female Sexuality' (1931) Freud wrote about the castration complex and the Oedipal situation for girls as follows:

> Quite different are the effects of the castration complex in the female. She acknowledges the fact of her castration, and with it, too, the superiority of the male and her own inferiority; but she rebels against this unwelcome state of affairs. From this divided attitude three lines of development open up. The first leads to a general revulsion from sexuality. The little girl, frightened by the comparison with boys, grows dissatisfied with her clitoris, and gives up her phallic activity and with it her sexuality in general as well as a good part of her masculinity in other fields. The second line leads her to cling with defiant self-assertiveness to her threatened masculinity. To an incredibly late age she clings to the hope of getting a penis some time. That hope becomes her life's aim; and the phantasy of being a man in spite of everything often persists as a formative factor over long periods. This 'masculinity complex' in women can also result in a manifest homosexual choice of object. Only if her development follows the third, very circuitous, path does she reach the final normal female attitude, in which she takes her father as her object and so finds her way to the feminine form of the Oedipus complex.[23]

This leads Freud into his assertion that women will take one or other of these paths of development depending on the nature of the pre-Oedipal relationship with their mothers, and by the degree of *active passive aims*

passive-active aims with which they are born. The same is true for boys who may take a passive attitude to their fathers, to aim to be his sexual object in place of mother, rather than to try to be active in relation to mother. Which they do in the Oedipal phase is affected by their constitutional balance between active and passive aims. This is difficult to know about because it is always affected by very early experiences of pleasure and pain in the early weeks and months of primary care.

The notion of bisexuality in males and females is central to psychoanalysis. It is taken from biology, but really comes to operate in psychoanalysis as a fundamental concept in the theory. The propositions Freud makes about women, and men, need to be understood in the context of this assumption of bisexuality. The resolution of the Oedipal situation for both sexes is affected by the perception of possession of a penis or not and the meaning this has for each boy or girl, and by the constitutional predisposition to seek active or passive pleasures. This predisposition is affected by the baby's early experience of passive or active pleasures. Before puberty bisexuality takes the form of seeking a mix of active or passive aims; only after puberty does bisexuality become expressed in genital ways in heterosexual and homosexual object relations.

Freud makes it quite clear that physical sexual characteristics do not parallel mental characteristics or sexual attitudes and behaviour. This is why he uses the distinction between active and passive and prefers this distinction to that of masculine and feminine which is too strongly linked to ideas of biological males and females.

The psychoanalytic theory of sexuality developed by Freud has provoked mixed responses since it first began to be published in 1905. It has always been attacked by some group or other – at first some Catholics and bourgeois politicians were offended by it, or said it was untrue that children were sexual before reaching pubescence. Later it was attacked by some analysts, Carl Jung being the first to develop a wider conception of libidinal energy than just sexual energy. Jung himself was prepared to use Freudian ideas with some patients for whom it seemed suitable so he claimed. Others have since abandoned what they came to see as the overemphasis on sexuality in Freudian theory.

In Freud's own lifetime the theory of sexuality as it applied to women was much criticized by women analysts and by some men.[24] More recently it has been attacked by some in the Women's Movement in the United States and Britain especially.

Political groups of the left and right have criticized psychoanalysis: for being Jewish – the Nazis burnt Freud's books – or for being bourgeois and reactionary by the Communist Party in the Soviet Union. The Communist Party of the Soviet Union has attacked psychoanalysis strongly in some periods. At other times it has ignored it as being irrelevant to wider political struggles.

Some groups have responded more positively. In the early days of the Russian Revolution, psychoanalysis was seen as a materialist view on which to base sexual reforms such as the availability of abortion, birth control, divorce and education for women, and for making homosexuality, especially that between men, legal. Some on the left have continued to use Freudian theory, especially groups in both the Women's Movement and in the Gay Movement. These people find that Freudian theory is not oppressive towards women, nor towards gays, in any intrinsic way.

The theory is an attempt to understand the variety of types of human sexualities and does *not* assume that everyone must conform to a particular conception of male or female gender roles, nor that everyone should or can follow the same sexual morality with regard to perversions or variation of sexual partners during the life cycle. The therapeutic practice is designed to aid men and women to suffer less, and the conceptualization of sexuality is developed from this basis of trying to lessen unnecessary suffering for women or men who have conflicts rooted in their psychosexual functioning. The aim of therapy is to reduce suffering by supporting some people to be different, not to conform to gender role conceptions and actions which are unsuitable for them. Women or gays in particular are not to be made to conform to conventional gender roles by psychotherapy – they may be aided to resolve their conflicts in other ways within therapy.

There is in Freud an uneasy relation between two areas of his theory about gender and sexuality. On the one hand he continually uses the notion of the basic bisexuality of humans which is sometimes expressed as the early infantile choice of active or passive pleasures and sometimes as the masculine and the feminine aspects of infant sexuality. For example girls are said to be 'masculine' if and when they masturbate; boys may take a passive 'feminine' attitude to their fathers. This idea of a fundamental bisexuality combines uneasily with Freud's statements about women or men, when he attaches more weight to the difference between the anatomy of the sexes. For instance, in his paper 'Some Psychical Consequences of the Anatomical Distinction between the Sexes' (1925) he writes:

> In girls the motive for the demolition of the Oedipus complex
> is lacking. Castration has already had its effect, which was to

force the child into the situation of the Oedipus complex. Thus the Oedipus complex escapes the fate which it meets with in boys: it may be slowly abandoned or dealt with by repression, or its effects may persist far into women's normal mental life. I cannot evade the notion (though I hesitate to give it expression) that for women the level of what is ethically normal is different from what it is in men. Their superego is never so inexorable, so impersonal, so independent of its emotional origins as we require it to be in men. Character-traits which critics of every epoch have brought up against women — that they show less sense of justice than men, that they are less ready to submit to the great exigencies of life, that they are more often influenced in their judgements by feelings of affection or hostility — all these would be amply accounted for by the modification in the formation of their superego which we have inferred above. We must not allow ourselves to be deflected from such conclusions by the denials of the feminists, who are anxious to force us to regard the two sexes as completely equal in position and worth; but we shall, of course, willingly agree that the majority of men are also far behind the masculine ideal and that all human individuals, as a result of their bisexual disposition and of cross-inheritance, combine in themselves both masculine and feminine characteristics, so that pure masculinity and femininity remain theoretical constructions of uncertain content.[25]

Freud admits that this is very tentative, and seemed to be aware that there was something amiss with what he was saying. There is something amiss and it is that he is trying to combine two theoretical positions together which are not really combinable.

The theory of bisexuality stresses that there are some similarities between boys and girls. This is especially so during the first two phases of development, the oral and the anal where the pleasures and pains are similar if not identical for both sexes. During the phallic phase there are similarities too — both enjoy stimulation of the genital area and both are interested in the penis (when girls play with little boys). The castration complex affects them differently — boys who have seen girls think it is a real threat that they can loose their penises while girls know they are without a penis but want one. Hence the two begin to diverge but not completely.

A theory which sets out from stressing the differences between the sexes tends to concentrate on adult men and women and to derive conclusions from them. Sometimes Freud writes as if all women are less ready to show a sense of justice than men, or to submit to the exigencies of life, or are over-emotional in their judgements, as in the above quotation. This sort of statement is incompatible with the bisexuality theory, for this latter stresses that there are no such generalizations as 'all women think or do x' which can be made. Nor can propositions such as 'all men think or do y' be made.

Freud seems to have become irrational at this point in his arguments with the feminists, and to have become less careful and professional in his writings. He is aware of this too — but still wrote and published such sentences as those just quoted and discussed, where Freud seems to assume that women are not 'completely equal in position and worth'.[26] He also says that most men fail to reach 'the masculine ideal' — whatever that is.

None of this should detract from a recognition of the major work Freud did achieve in the rational understanding of human sexuality and of infant sexuality, and its relationship with problems in achieving some sense of well-being among adults.

LATER DEVELOPMENTS IN THE STUDY OF SOCIALIZATION

There have been numerous developments within psychoanalysis since Freud wrote about the process of socialization from a psychoanalytic point of view. These have extended the number of key stages in the socialization process in both the pre-Oedipal and post-Oedipal phases. The work of Melanie Klein and psychoanalysts in the British object-relations school has stressed the first year of life, even the first few months after birth, because at this stage very fundamental processes occur to do with a baby gaining a fundamental sense of 'being-in-the-world' which is derived from 'good-enough mothering' in Winnicott's phrase. Without this stage being lived through satisfactorily by the baby the seeds not of neurosis, but of psychosis, may be found.

This perspective is a much-needed corrective to the wilder side of the sociology of deviance derived from the labelling perspective. When taken to extremes this perspective suggested that madness did not really exist, that extreme forms of mental illness in which reality is highly distorted were only the product of labels being applied by the psychiatric profession to other people who just had different versions of reality to those of the bourgeoisie, or the Party elite in the case of the Soviet Union's psychiatric practices. This perspective overlooked the suffering of the mentally ill themselves which they often see as being inside themselves and not the result of how they are treated by others. The work of psychoanalysts on the first year or so of life has helped to deepen knowledge about how some people fail to develop a basic sense of being at home in the world, a basic sense of trust of other people. The labelling perspective did lead to some achievements in various spheres of deviance, for example in showing how hospitalization of the mentally ill could be seen as reinforcing or even creating some incapacities in the patients. It has been too impatient with the newer forms of psychoanalytic perspectives on early infancy and the effects poor socialization at this stage can have on the grown-up person.

The work of Jacques Lacan has played a part in the deepening of psychoanalytic understandings of early socialization. His work on the phase he termed the *mirror phase*, which starts with self-recognition in a mirror at six to eight months, and continues to develop the child's recognition of others until two years of age, has parallels with the work just mentioned done in Britain. Young children learn to understand themselves as a *whole* entity when they see themselves in a mirror. The first mirror they learn from is, however, the face of their mother who reflects back to the baby the pleasure she has in them.[27]

Psychoanalysts and social psychologists have also been concerned with extending the study of socialization into later periods of childhood, adolescence, and young adulthood. It needs to be remembered that some of Freud's patients were young adults, but that he tended to go back to the first five years of life, and especially to the Oedipus phase of development in understanding these young people. Others since have seen later phases of life as having their own specific tasks. In the work of Erik Erikson, for instance, this is most developed. Erikson has a series of eight stages of development, the first five of which are developments of Freud's oral, anal, phallic (which Erikson calls locomotor-genital) latency and genital (which for Erikson is puberty and adolescence as it was in Freud basically). To these Erikson added *young adulthood* — in which the main task centres on establishing relationships (intimacy versus isolation as Erikson puts it). [28]

He also added *adulthood* in which the main tasks centre around generativity or stagnation — contributing to the socialization of the next generation through parenting or teaching, and to cultural development, versus stagnating into an uncreative, sterile middle age. The mid-life crisis has been developed as a notion by others than Erikson, but there is here a common concern with the problems of the second half of life, stemming initially from Carl Jung. Freud seemed very impatient with people at this stage — forty or so was about the latest age he thought people would be helped by therapy. Jung and others have since proved otherwise. There is undoubtedly an important market force working here — for people in full adulthood and middle age usually have more time and *money* to spend on psychotherapy. Psychotherapists, especially in the United States, but elsewhere too, have had to respond to this market to find clients who can pay. This necessitated the development of psychoanalytic ideas about adulthood. A recent book by the sociologist Neil Smelser and Erik Erikson (editors) *Themes of Love and Work in Adulthood* (1980) has developed this area further. [29]

This theme is linked with Erikson's final stage: *maturity* in which the main task is ego integrity versus despair. This concerns the problems associated with coping with the last few decades of life, when children have left home, and paid work may be ending. It is linked with the way in which a person has come through all the earlier phases, for each phase in this kind of theory affects later ones. Tasks which have remained unresolved at an earlier phase recur with later crisis points in the life-cycle.

Erikson's work on youth and identity crises has been used in textbooks in social psychology and in some in sociology. His ideas have influenced many researchers in history who have developed psychoanalytically informed studies of historical figures, following Erikson's own studies in psychohistory as this work is called. Erikson has written on *The Young Man Luther* and *Gandhi*. Sociologists are usually very critical of this work because it overemphasizes the individual and underplays the importance of class and structural factors in the making of history. From the perspective of Freudian social theory the work of Erikson and others is interesting, but disappointing in its failure to use or develop the social theory in Freudian theory and over-concentrating on personalities.

THE FAMILY

A major criticism which anthropologists and sociologists have made of Freud's theory of socialization, a criticism which began with Malinowski's research on the Trobriand Islanders, has been that the theory only fits those societies which have a nuclear family. This criticism makes the point that Freud's theory of socialization makes the Oedipus phase central, but that this Oedipal complex of feelings is only applicable to nuclear families in which the children are reared by their biological parents, who continue to live together and to have sexual relations with one another, after the children are born. This is an intense situation for the child, as Freud makes clear, because the child's rival for erotic attentions is also a parent figure, a socializing agent. Among the Trobrianders, but by no means only among them, the child may have someone else, such as mother's brother, that is the child's uncle, as his or her main socializing agent. Mother's lover, who may or may not be the child's biological father, and of whom the child is jealous for erotic reasons, is not the same person who arouses the child's anger by saying 'No' to its wishes as the main socializing agent has to do.

Since Malinowski developed this kind of argument further research has made it clear that the infant Trobriander is socialized by mother and a father who is also mother's lover in the first few years of life, up to and beyond the typical age of Oedipus. The uncle only takes over as a socializing agent when the child can talk and walk. Anger is expressed towards the uncle by children in the Trobriand Islands, and later observers think some of this is displaced from the child's father in any case. There are, therefore, Oedipal triangles for both boys and girls in Trobriand society — the father is the son's rival for mother and the mother is the daughter's rival for father.

> Psychoanalysts and social scientists who reject its universality have generally based their position on Malinowski's study of the Trobriand Islanders, discussed on this question in *Sex and Repression in Savage Society*, (1927) . . .
>
> . . . Basically what Malinowski — and other anthropologists focusing on the matrilineal clan structure of such societies as the Trobriands — missed was that in all of these societies there is in fact a nuclear family consisting of mother, father (her mate), and children, and that the father — not the mother's brother — is the sexual possessor of the mother, therefore the sexual rival for the mother, to the boy. Similarly, with father and mother possessing each other, exclusively, in the girl's sexual longing for the father, the mother is obviously the crucial sexual rival. Thus there will inevitably be Oedipal triangles. [30]

GENDER AND SEXUALITY

(a) Women

Both male and female psychoanalysts have changed Freud's theory of femininity, both during his own lifetime and since he died. While staying within mainstream psychoanalysis Melanie Klein stressed the importance of pre-Oedipal experiences for boys and girls, but she stressed the infant girl's pre-Oedipal relationship with her mother far more than

Freud had done. The feelings of hate towards mother are projected out onto a bad mother figure by the girl, only to be taken in again. Girls could have a pre-Oedipal superego which later developed into a severe superego, more severe than in males, because the feelings of hate towards mother, the first love and hate object for all babies, were reinforced at the Oedipal stage by rivalrous feelings between mother and daughter. In Freud's work the superego was thought of as weaker, not stronger, in women than in men.[31]

The work of Klein on early object-relations which was carried out in the nineteen-twenties and nineteen-thirties, and elaborated later, forms the foundations upon which the post-Second World War 'English School' of psychoanalysts have built and developed. This does not mean that the 'English School' of psychoanalysis is entirely Kleinian — it is not. It does mean that the work both Melanie Klein and Anna Freud did on children in the first months and years of life has had a major impact on later discussions within psychoanalysis. The emphasis is much more on pre-Oedipal emotions, and on seeing Oedipus as being earlier in life.[32]

There is evidence too, from other social scientists, that parents relate to baby boys and girls differently from birth, and that gender identity begins much earlier than Freud's Oedipus stage at around the age of three. Infants have often acquired pre-verbal understandings about gender differences according to some analysts, and certainly acquire an understanding of gender as they learn to speak. The first words of many, if not all babies, are 'mama' and 'dada' or their equivalents. From this basic vocabulary understandings of gender begin — the baby is the same gender as, or the opposite gender to, mother.

This later work would form some challenge to Freud's assumption that infants all assume that boys and girls are the same in that all have penises, as do mothers as well as fathers. The problem here is being clear about the age of children being discussed, for Freud they were three- to five-year-olds who can speak, whereas other analysts are talking about much younger infants. The whole discussion can become impossible to resolve because the sources of the evidence are so varied, and restricted to the sample of cases and children particular analysts, or groups of analysts, have seen. Analysts are trying to conceptualize the meanings male and female anatomies acquire for particular individuals and groups. The meanings can and do vary. The amount of variation in meanings across cultures is disputed by sociologists, anthropologists, and psychoanalysts. The range of possible meanings is very great for those who maintain that the anatomical differences between the sexes do not entail any specific roles for men and women; and is restricted for those who think that the range is limited in major ways. No society for instance has ever defined primary care of babies as a task for men — but this should be possible if those writers are right who maintain that culture could define things this way. Women are always involved in primary child care in all cultures, even if men are equally involved too. Men have not so far ever taken over full time responsibility for the tasks of primary baby care. This may be beginning to happen in a few cases in some advanced societies, but is unlikely to become a general pattern in the near future. The reasons are partly to do with the difficulties of change in such an area of unconscious meaning as that of gender. Masculinity, which even for modern men who are liberal on many social and political issues, including women's liberation, at least in the abstract, may not include full-time care of babies and households.

The unconscious meanings for women of having a baby are not changed easily either. Most women will not change their unconscious understandings of either femininity, or indeed of masculinity, as a result of rational discourse. Those women who can feel fulfilled without children would do so anyway, quite independently of any social scientific 'findings' about gender role differentiation across a wide variety of cultures. Psychoanalysis can provide a way of conceptualizing how some women emerge from their socialization and Oedipal phases with an unconscious desire for a baby, and some do not. There need not be any implication that one of these outcomes is better morally, politically, or psychologically than the other. (The same point can be made about psychoanalytic conceptualizations of homosexuality and its genesis. Understanding how some people emerge preferring only same sex objects and others do not does not imply anything about evaluations of a moral, political, or psychological kind.)

The unconscious meanings of gender differences are difficult to handle in rational discourse in any case. The literature on the subject, starting with Freud's own works on femininity and the psychology of women, has illustrated the difficulties of being rational in an area such as this. There are at least two kinds of unconscious group process which affect this type of discourse. On the one hand there are male psychoanalysts, including in some of his writings Freud himself, who seem to take on the role of preserving the archaic heritage. At times psychoanalysts and sociologists can seem to be supporting the traditional Western understandings of the roles appropriate to men and women: men are more physically aggressive than women; they fight more than women; women are more emotional than rational in their dealings with other people; women care for others, especially children, the sick and the old, more than men; men are more inclined to be

promiscuous sexually than are women. These are some of the components of the traditional Western views of the differences between the
two genders. They are sometimes to be found in writings from people
claiming to be influenced by psychoanalysis. Usually it is psychoanalysis
with its social theory removed which is used and which enables the
person to ignore the ways in which they may be being unwittingly
used to *maintain* the archaic definitions and understandings of gender
and to avoid *analysing* this very process.

The other aspect of group process is the one found in the psychoanalysis of crowds — the hatred of outsiders, and of those who hold
different views; the uncritical repeating of certain verbal slogans in a
non-rational way; the maintenance of forced equality among group
members and intolerance of the opposition; and the narcissism of
minor differences. All these unconscious phenomena, which form a part
of psychoanalytical social theory as developed by Freud, affect the
conduct of discussions among and with feminists, or other groups
with a particular identity formed around sexuality, such as some gay
liberation groups. This is very unfortunate in that it has led to non-
rational opposition to psychoanalysis among some of these movements
of social-cultural change when they could have used and extended
psychoanalytic ideas and practices for their own work. This has happened
in a few exceptional cases.[33] (Juliet Mitchell; Mario Meili; Herbert
Marcuse).

One of the consequences of these unconscious processes is a
distortion of what psychoanalysis is, and of how it could potentially
contribute to the theory and practice of contemporary changes in
gender and sexuality. Discussions in this area have rarely set out from a
clear understanding of Freudian social theory. This theory could be
developed further and enriched if it was taken as a starting point. One
of the few people to do so was Herbert Marcuse in *Eros and Civilization* (1955). This text is in turn founded on work done by Adorno
and Horkheimer in developing the understanding of Freud within the
context of critical theory. This understanding of Freudian theory
was one based on taking the instinct-theory seriously and not trying
to remove it as Fromm and Horney, for example, tried to do. Sociologists both before and since the work of these critical theorists have
tried to introduce societal and cultural variation into psychoanalytic
work to such an extent that the central focus on unconscious processes
of repression and on the universal aspects of the instinctual drive theory
is lost.

Marcuse did retain the notion of repression of instinctual drives as
being a central one for Freudian critical social theory. He did, however,

add
marcure Civil'3
Eros + to 52.

try to make it more historically variable than the social theory of Freud had been. Marcuse introduced the notion of *surplus repression* to conceptualize the idea that there could be more repression of polymorphous perverse infant sexuality than was needed to maintain modern technologically advanced societies such as the United States in the nineteen-fifties. Surplus repression was the amount of repression that was over and above that needed to maintain a reasonable standard of living in any given historical era. There was, however, a process occurring which could be mistaken for undoing repression, namely that of sexuality being used for stimulating consumption of goods produced in modern capitalist societies. For example, the use of attractive girls in advertisements to sell cars, the promise of a false kind of satisfaction of infantile desires in many food advertisements, or the appeal to narcissism in selling clothes and make-up to women. Marcuse saw this kind of use of sexuality to sell things as a form of what he called *repressive desublimation* because it remained a repressive form of consumption in so far as people needed to work for money to buy goods which did not satisfy the consumer's instinctual desires in any case.

(b) The Gay Movement

The movement towards 'feminization' of culture and society which the Women's Movement and the Gay Movement could be seen as aiming for was not repressive desublimation in the first instance. Marcuse thought some aspects of both movements had lost their initial aims and impetus towards this goal, however. The Gay Movement has in part become the basis of a new consumer industry aimed at the surplus money of gay people who can buy clothes and holidays, for instance, on a scale which is higher than their counterparts who are married and supporting children. This new form of gay capitalism can also be seen as a protection too, because in societies like those of the West an infrastructure of gay consumerism of all kinds, whatever its drawbacks, does help to maintain a gay presence and identity in an environment that sometimes does become hostile to gays. The consumer-based gay industries are a form of protection against the movements of traditionalists to re-assert the taboo on homosexuality, especially among men.

The Gay Movement has been antagonistic towards psychoanalysis until recently.[34] Many gay people still think that psychoanalysis sees them as 'sick'. This view fails to do justice to the way Freud altered the prevailing views of the distinction between sickness and normality, stressing as he did the continuities between the two. It also fails to see that in Freudian analysis heterosexuality is never complete — there are always some deires in the unconscious for the parent of the same sex, and for other people of the same sex. This does not mean that the desires are acknowledged, or acted upon. Those who do act on their homosexual impulses may save themselves from neurosis, just as those who act on perverse heterosexual impulses will avoid neuroses created by instinctual erotic impulses which are repressed but strong.

However, there is some reason to think that many analysts, and some psychotherapists, do have a negative attitude towards male homosexuals, sometimes both in theory and in practice. Wilhelm Reich, seen posthumously as a sexual liberationist in the nineteen-sixties and early nineteen-seventies, refused to take male homosexuals as patients and saw genital heterosexuality as the ideal. Homosexuality was a negative consequence of religious anti-sexual moral systems for Reich. It was not treated as a fundamental aspect of all unconscious desire in human beings, but as a distortion of 'real' sexual desire which Reich treated as being naturally heterosexual.[35] Carl Jung was also reportedly against having male homosexuals as patients, and his theory, although incorporating a bisexual dimension in the concepts of anima (in men) and animus (in women) moved away explicitly from Freud's emphasis on sexuality and the body's instinctual desires.[36]

The sociological analysis provided by symbolic interactionism gave theoretical legitimation for the practices of gay counselling and and be-friending services set up by gay people in nearly every large town and city in Britain, Western Europe and North America. This has been an important achievement psychotherapeutically. Symbolic interactionists do not see meanings as *fixed,* once and for all, by biology nor even by socialization. Meanings are flexible.

There has been a great gain for many individuals of all ages, but especially the young, in the interaction with other gay people who have a positive attitude to their own homosexual desires. Much unnecessary guilt and anxiety has been removed from many people's lives through the growth of a gay sub-culture in Western societies. There are, however, some problem areas remaining which seem to need theoretical ideas not provided by symbolic interactionism, and which the existence of a gay sub-culture does not resolve in practice. [37]

The initial benefits of the gay sub-cultures' existence are now taken for granted by many, but there are still problems of depression, loneliness, promiscuity, lack of relationships for some gays — these are problems as defined by gays themselves. In these areas gay counselling is of some help, but often those who contact the services are those who are least overwhelmed by their problems. There are problems, for example, for married gay men and women, which are partly induced by the lack of support in the gay sub-culture towards married gays and bisexuals. They are often perceived as parasitical, and using other gays for sexual purposes only, relying on their families for their personal relationships. Any problems with the police are very distressing for these men, and yet it is married men who are more likely than other gays to 'cruise' for casual sex in public places, and who often run greater risks with the police than do gays who live alone, or with other gay people, and use their own beds for sexual encounters.

Psychoanalytic theory and associated practices have application to these problems. It can move beyond describing different sub-cultures and their attitudes and values towards the homosexual role, and begin to conceptualize an explanation of these phenomena. Although such attempts to explain may not of themselves change the situation immediately, they are the necessary prerequisites for change.

In particular, the psychoanalytic theorization of the range of sexual desires, and of aggression, can encompass the above problem areas into a theoretical framework which explains their major aspects. For Freud, but not for many of his followers since, including as noted above, Reich, men and women are not biologically given as heterosexual beings. That is it is an accomplishment of socialization to produce men and women who are genitally heterosexual in their desires; this is not given as a basic datum of human biology.

The notion of infantile, polymorphous, bi-sexuality is fundamental here. One could say that the existence of adult homosexuals, and bisexuals, is no more surprising on this view than that of heterosexuals. The existence of adult celibates is no more or less surprising than that of promiscuous adults.

The publication of Guy Hocquenghem's *Homosexual Desire* in French in 1972, and in English in 1978, changed the relation of some gays to psychoanalysis.[38] In this book Hocquenghem uses the category 'desire' derived from Freud, via Lacan and others. He interrogates the texts in which Freud discusses male homosexuality and points to the assumption of polymorphous bisexuality in the unconscious and the assumption that deflected homosexual libido can be and is used for the maintenance of social bonds.

Sociology, especially the sociology of deviance developed by symbolic interactionists and labelling theorists, can show those psychoanalysts and therapists who see male homsexuality as something to oppose in therapeutic practice, by various means, usually implicit and indirect, that they may be being influenced by particular cultural norms and values. Equally, psychoanalysis need not be seen as 'anti-gay', or as perpetuating the taboo on male homosexuality, by sociologists, or gay activists, but rather as trying to provide a theoretically conceived explanation of the taboo itself.

The taboo on male homosexuality can be seen as part of the sublimation of all forms of direct expression of sexuality of any kind. However, it has a particular strength and form in some societies, at particular historical periods, because their major institutions are concerned with producing and re-producing a dedication to work, and men who will fight, kill and be killed, in the armed forces.

Freud's work on gender and sexuality provides the foundations for a critical theory of patriarchal societies' definitions of gender roles and moral values around sexuality and aggression. He does not provide a justification for these, as some critics have claimed, but a theoretical account of them. Freud's theory aims to show that gender roles and morality are not based on biology, or upon natural law, as patriarchal ideologies have claimed. Rather they are based on human cultures' unconscious archaic heritage. This is difficult to change, but not as impossible as a fact of nature would be.

NOTES AND REFERENCES

[1] S. Freud and J. Breuer, *Studies on Hysteria,* Standard Edition, Volume 2, Hogarth Press, London (1955), (first published 1893–5).

[2] S. Freud, *The Interpretation of Dreams,* Standard Edition, Volume 4 and 5, Hogarth Press, London (1958), (first published 1900).

[3] Ibid, Chapter VI.

[4] See, for example, J. Lacan, *The Four Fundamental Concepts of Psychoanalysis,* Chapter 2, translated by A. Sheridan, Hogarth Press, London (1977).

[5] H. Stuart Hughes, *Consciousness and Society. The Reorientation of European Social thought 1890-1930, MacGibbon & Kee, London (1967), pp. 133-4.*

[6] S. Freud, *Three Essays on the Theory of Sexuality,* Standard Edition, Volume 7, Hogarth Press, London (1953), p. 168.

[7] S. Freud, *The Unconscious,* Standard Edition, Volume 14, Hogarth Press, London (1963), p. 177.

[8] S. Freud, *Three Essays on the Theory of Sexuality,* Standard Edition, Volume 7, Hogarth Press, London (1953); and The Pelican Freud Library, Volume 7 *On Sexuality,* Harmondsworth, Penguin (1977), p. 45 (the essays were first published 1905).

[9] Ibid., p. 82.

[10] Ibid., p. 74.

[11] D. Wrong, *The Oversocialized Conception of Man in Modern Sociology*, originally published in *American Sociological Review*, Vol. 26, No. 2 (April 1961), pp. 183-93.

[12] See S. Freud and J. Breuer, *Studies on Hysteria*, Part IV.

[13] See, for example, S. Freud, *On the Sexual Theories of Children*, Standard Edition, Volume 9, Hogarth Press, London (1959); and The Pelican Freud Library, Volume 7, *On Sexuality*, Penguin, Harmondsworth (1977).

[14] S. Freud, *The Sexual Enlightenment of Children* (1907), Standard Edition, Volume 9, Hogarth Press, London (1959).

[15] Ibid.

[16] Ibid. Reference *An Introduction to Sociology*, edited by R. Bocock *et al.*, Fontana/Collins, London (1980), p. 61.

[17] R. Bocock *et al.*, op. cit., p. 61.

[18] S. Freud, *Three Essays on the Theory of Sexuality*, Standard Edition, Volume 7, Hogarth Press, London (1953), p. 187.

[19] S. Freud, *The Interpretation of Dreams*, Standard Edition, Volumes 4 and 5, Hogarth Press, London (1958). The relevant discussion is in Chapter V, section D, Beta, 'Dreams of the death of persons of whom a dreamer is fond'.

[20] S. Freud, *The Psychogenesis of a Case of Homosexuality in a Woman* (1920), Standard Edition, Volume 18, Hogarth Press, London (1955); and The Pelican Freud Library, Volume 9, *Case Histories II*, Penguin, Harmondsworth (1979), p. 380, note 1.

[21] S. Freud, 'Female Sexuality', Standard Edition, Volume 21, Hogarth Press, London (1961); and The Pelican Freud Library, Volume 7, *On Sexuality*, Penguin, Harmondsworth (1977).

[22] See S. Freud, *Three Essays on the Theory of Sexuality* (1905), Essay II, Section 5, 'The Sexual Researches of Childhood', The Pelican Freud Library, Volume 7, Penguin, Harmondsworth (1977), pp. 112-15.

[23] S. Freud, 'Female Sexuality', The Pelican Freud Library, Volume 7, *On Sexuality*, Penguin, Harmondsworth (1977), p. 376.

[24] See H. Nagera (editor), *Basic Psychoanalytic Concepts on the Libido Theory*, The Hampstead Clinic Psychoanalytic Library, Volume 1, Allen & Unwin, London (1969), sections on: Bisexuality; Activity-Passivity; Masculinity-Femininity, especially, p. 133.

[25] See S. Freud, 'Female Sexuality' (1931), The Pelican Freud Library, Volume 7, *On Sexuality,* Penguin, Harmondsworth (1977), p. 342.

[26] Ibid., p. 342.

[27] J. Lacan, *Ecrits. A Selection,* translated by A. Sheridan, Tavistock Publications, London (1977), pp. 1–7.

[28] E. Erikson, *Childhood and Society,* Hogarth Press, London (1965), and W. W. Norton, New York (1950), see especially Chapter 7, 'Eight Ages of Man'.

[29] N. Smelser and E. Erikson, *Themes of Love and Work in Adulthood,* Grant McIntyre, London (1980) and Harvard, USA (1980).

[30] R. Endleman, *Psyche and Society: Explorations in Psychoanalytic Sociology,* Columbia University Press, New York, (1981), pp. 25–6.

[31] See H. Segal, *Introduction to The Work Of Melanie Klein,* W. Heinemann, London (1964).

[32] See N. Chodorow, *The Reproduction of Mothering: Psychoanalysis and the Sociology of Gender,* Berkeley University Press, California (1978). This book gives a useful overview of the English School of Psychoanalysis, written by someone with a sociological awareness. It is discussed in Chapter 4 of this book.

[33] J. Mitchell, *Psychoanalysis and Feminism,* Penguin, Harmondsworth (1974). This remains a seminal text in its area.

[34] See M. Mieli, *Homosexuality and Liberation; Elements of a Gay Critique,* translated by D. Fernbach, Gay Men's Press, London (1980). First published in Italian, 1977.

[35] G. Rycroft, *Reich,* Fontana Modern Masters, London (1971), p.63.

[36] A. Storr, *Jung,* Fontana Modern Masters, London (1973), p.54.

[37] See K. Plummer, *Sexual Stigma: an interactionist account,* Routledge & Kegan Paul, London (1975), and also K. Plummer (editor), *The Making of the Modern Homosexual,* Hutchinson, London (1981).

[38] G. Hocquenghem, *Homosexual Desire,* English translation, Allison and Busby, London (1978).

3

Freud's Social Theory

Freud's social theory has two main levels of analysis in it — the cultural and the social-structural. It is a theory about beliefs, value systems and symbols at the level of culture, and about authority relations and aggression at the level of social structure.

Psychoanalytic social theory is not like other theories about social groups in sociology. The reason for this is that it is a theory about emotions and the ways in which they are produced, reproduced and about how they affect the social actions of people. As it is a part of psychoanalysis this theory of emotions is about *unconscious* emotions, rather than conscious ones. It is assumed that the unconscious is the root structure which affects the more superficial level of consciousness. This is a working assumption, fully vindicated in Freud's view in the light of his use and development of it in therapeutic work. This is not to say that Freud thought he had confirmed his social theory as a whole within clinical practice, for this would be impossible. He regarded the assumption that there is an area of unconscious emotion underlying the conscious level, and that this unconscious level may influence individuals and groups when they are unaware of it, as being fundamental.

To understand the main strands of Freud's social theory it is necessary to consider what may seem an obscure part of psychoanalytic ideas – namely the death instincts. Far from being irrelevant to the theory of groups and of cultural values, the concept of the death instincts is central. This concept is used, for example, in the way Freud came to conceptualize the work of the superego, as will be shown below. This innovation within psychoanalytic theory is added to the work Freud had done in the first part of his career on sexuality. It does need to be brought into the discussions of psychoanalysis and sociology more than has been done recently by many writers.

THE DEATH INSTINCTS

Although Freud had been concerned with the human propensity to kill other humans, or to wish to kill them, from the inception of his work in psychoanalysis in *The Interpretation of Dreams* (1900) and in *Totem and Taboo* (1912-13) it was not until 1920 in *Beyond the Pleasure Principle* that he first put forward the notion of the death instincts as such.[1] Throughout the whole of his development of psychoanalysis Freud retained the concept of the sexual instincts which he had developed in the first decade of his work. He also retained the basic idea of there being two sets of instincts, but whereas one might say that the first formulation of the two instincts was that they were both positive in their effects, the second formulation depended more on a contrast between positive and negative. In the first formulation Freud posited the notion of the ego, or self-preservative, instincts in addition to the sexual instincts. In the second he added the death instincts as a source of negative, destructive, energy in place of the ego instincts. These latter were subsumed under the revised conceptualization of the sexual instincts taking either the self, ego, or an external object or person as the objective for satisfaction of their desire.

Freud's reasons for introducing the death instincts were connected with three areas of interest to him:

(1) Therapy with two types of patients focused Freud's attention on the need for some addition to the pleasure principle, or a move beyond it. There were first the soldiers suffering from war neuroses. These men dreamt of the situation in which they were 'shell-shocked' or wounded and not of themselves as healthy either physically or emotionally. By doing this they were repeating a painful situation, not dreaming in a way which would fulfil the wish to be well again, as the pleasure principle would lead the analyst to expect. Secondly, there were patients who repeated painful emotions in relation to their analyst which they had first experienced with their parents. Some of these

patients did not seem to want to get well but there seemed to be a strong unconscious force operating to keep them ill. Freud had assumed that there was a strong wish in the unconscious to gain pleasure and to reduce painful experiences, and that the unconscious always operated on this pleasure principle. These two phenomena were puzzling and seemed to require a revision of the concept of the unconscious pleasure principle. There seemed to be some other unconscious factor at work in these cases — namely a *compulsion to repeat* painful situations.[2]

(2) The First World War had posed serious issues for all European thinkers, writers, artists, political philosophers, and for Freud too. By the end of the war in 1918 Freud had become convinced that he needed to be able to understand within a psychoanalytic framework of theory and concepts how this kind of organized human violence against others was possible. Even if he did not entirely succeed in explaining the war to the satisfaction of most political historians — something he was not in fact trying to do — he did find that again there seemed to be an unconscious emotional satisfaction involved for the nations fighting one another. The sense of elation experienced by the British, the Germans and the French at the outbreak of the war, and the inability of anyone to stop the carnage in the trenches, suggested to Freud that there was some unconscious satisfaction involved in the war for the nations taking part which could not be explained by the psychoanalytic idea that the unconscious always seeks to maximize pleasure and to minimize pain. Freud's revisions to his theory were therefore partly carried out so that the fact that early twentieth-century history in Europe failed to follow the smooth pursuit of happiness promised by nineteenth-century progress theories of historical development could be accommodated.[3]

The psychoanalytic interpretation of history has had an importance because other theories of history are rooted in the nineteenth century when progress of some kind was assumed. Liberalism, Marxism, socialism, and conservatism all have their roots in this period prior to the two world wars of this century — wars of a kind which affected everyone in ways which no previous type of warfare in history had done.

(3) Religious rituals of sacrifice. Religions throughout the world have ritual sacrifices as a central component of their symbol systems. This had first fascinated Freud in relation to totemism, and the sacrifice of the totemic animal among those groups which had an animal as a totem. He had provided a different explanation from Durkheim of totemism, and totemic sacrifices. (Durkheim's study of totemism, *The Elementary Forms of the Religious Life,* was published in 1912,

the same year that Freud first published part of the text now known as *Totem and Taboo*. Freud makes a number of references to Durkheim's works in the second part which was published in 1913.)

Freud had argued in *Totem and Taboo* that the totem animal was a symbol for the primal father — an unconscious primal father. This father was killed by rebellious sons, the band of brothers, because he forbade them access to the women. Totem animals were symbols of the primal father, just as animals could symbolize aspects of the father of a child that were hated. Little Hans, the boy who was analysed in the case history 'Analysis of a phobia in a five-year-old boy' (1909) had had a phobia about horses which was explained by Freud by assuming that the horses were a symbol of the father. In dreams too, animals often symbolize aspects of parental figures. Other religions also use animal sacrifices, as in Hinduism for example.

By 1920 Freud was becoming interested in developing the psycho-analytic theory of European religions — Christianity and Judaism — something he was to do over the next two decades. The presence of killing animals in rituals of sacrifice needed some explanation, as did the 'killing' of Jesus in the rituals of Catholic Christianity. Again a move beyond the pleasure principle seemed to be required if this was to be done.

Beyond the Pleasure Principle (1920) is not an easy text. The main reason is that the arguments Freud produces hardly seem to justify the assertion of a notion as momentous as that of the death instincts. The reasons given for the introduction of them in this text are not very strong ones. For example, *the compulsion to repeat* is introduced first of all in relation to children's play, and to their liking to hear the same story read to them again and again. Here, however, Freud says that the pleasure principle and the reality principle are enough to explain these phenomena. Children are aiming to repeat pleasures by hearing a story a number of times because they have not yet learned that in reality there are many new stories, and that novelty can add to their pleasure as it does for adults.

The compulsion to repeat painful emotions and actions on the part of patients in therapy is not of this type. Here is something else operating which is more elementary, more primitive, more instinctual. It is the desire to return to an earlier state of things. This Freud calls 'the *conservative* nature of living substance' which aims to return to an inorganic state. This is how Freud tries to connect the observed compulsions to repeat pain with a strong instinctual drive to return to the inorganic; to die. The path to death is circuitous and indirect rather than being intelligently pursued by an organism and this Freud treats as a mark of its instinctual nature.[4]

The sexual instincts aim to preserve life and are in conflict with the other instincts of death in the individual and in the species. The sexual instincts can be repressed in some people and their energy re-used and sublimated into creative work and ethical actions. There is no complete satisfaction in this because there is always a gap between the pleasure demanded by the sexual instincts and the pleasure achieved through sublimated activities. Nevertheless this is the way in which human societies have developed and progressed to the level of civilization they have so far. Freud introduces the term Eros in *Beyond the Pleasure Principle* to describe the way the sexual instincts can be used to 'combine organic substances into ever larger unities'.[5]

These ideas were developed by Freud in his later writings on society and on religion. They are used by some other social theorists, especially Herbert Marcuse in his book *Eros and Civilization*.

Freud admitted that the arguments he used in *Beyond the Pleasure Principle,* which relied on biological research to establish that the notion of the death instincts which he was developing was not in opposition to biology and might even be supported by such research, were weak. They could be refuted by later research within biology. He seemed to be unsure also of how far he could use psychoanalytic research from clinical work to substantiate the notion of the death instincts at first. As time went by Freud seemed to be more secure in his view that the death instinct — life instinct opposition was a useful one to make in psychoanalytic theory for both therapeutic purposes and for developing the more social aspects of the theory. This became true of the way he developed his analysis of the ego and the part of the ego he termed the *superego*.

THE SUPEREGO

In trying to understand Freud's theory it is necessary to grasp that it was undergoing constant changes during Freud's working life. There is not, therefore, one single definitive version of psychoanalytic theory but a series of changes from the early works to the later ones.

The emergence of the concept of the death instincts was a major event in the development of the theory. Psychoanalytic theory can be divided roughly into two major phases:

Phase one — the work on sexual instincts and the ways in which they can be repressed, sublimated, acted on in perversions, form dream symbols or produce symptoms. This first phase was from 1895 to 1919.

Phase two – the work on the death instincts and the changes this led to in the understanding of the sexual instincts. This second phase of the theory produced the major contribution Freud made to the psychoanalytic theory of social groups and societies' values, religious beliefs and rituals, and authority structures. This second phase lasted from 1920 until 1939.

The emergence of the concept of the superego can be traced back to the early *Studies on Hysteria* and *The Interpretation of Dreams* where it appeared as the notion of a *censor* which forbids certain thoughts, wishes or desires. These censored ideas form *the repressed* part of the unconscious. There was also a second major idea that the concept of the superego picked up, namely the idea of the ego-ideal. The ego-ideal is set up in the young child's mind as a replacement for the infant's primary narcissism and represents an ideal image of how the person thinks they should be. For example, a child could have the idea that they should ideally be clever at school, good at sports, loving to parents, physically attractive, and be a brilliant musician. These ideals operate to spur a child or young adult to try to achieve as much as possible, but they are ideals which can never be attained in full.

In the text belonging to the second phase of Freud's work, *The Ego and the Id* (1923), a new model of the structure of the mind is outlined.[6] The reasons for needing some new conceptualization of the structure of the mind were both clinical ones and theoretical. Clinically there were paranoiac delusions to be explained. In the case history of Judge Schreber (1911) Freud had found it necessary to assume that a part of a person's mind could become split off, as it were, and keep watch over the rest of the person's thoughts and actions. Judge Schreber had thought that someone else was watching him; Freud interpreted this as a part of the Judge's own mind unconsciously appearing like this to him.

Theoretically the notion of the unconscious was unclearly related to that of consciousness. At first it had seemed that a part of the mind was conscious and did the work of repression, or censoring. But even in dreams it was apparent that the work of the censor could continue unconsciously. The puzzle may be stated in the following way. It is assumed that there are two main aspects to the mind of human beings, one aspect is consciousness and the other is unconcious. The unconcious contains the repressed wishes and desires that the conscious part rejects. Some of the work of censoring which wishes and desires are to be repressed or rejected is done while being asleep, that is it is done as an unconscious process.

So not all the work of censoring is done at the level of consciousness. How is it done unconciously? A part of the mind must be able to function as a repressing agent within the unconscious, so the unconscious is not just made up of repressed materials and the conscious is not the repressing agency.

Freud had asserted in the second edition of *Beyond the Pleasure Principle* which appeared in 1921 that 'It is certain that much of the ego is itself unconscious'. Here 'ego' is used as a term for what would have been called 'consciousness' because it would be absurd to say that consciousness is unconscious in large part. The ego is never wholly unconscious either. It is the aspect of the mind's functioning which is responsible for reality testing, that is for rational thinking, and for checking what it is safe to do in a given physical and social environment.

By introducing the term 'superego' in 1923 Freud was able to conceptualize the dual work of the earlier notion of ego. The superego becomes the censor; it can carry out this work of censorship either consciously or unconsciously. It also becomes the part of the mind which carries the ego-ideal and which criticizes the failure of the person to live up to these ideals. This critical function of the superego is taken over from parents, especially from the father. Children, especially boys and to a lesser extent most girls, resolve their conflicts around this Oedipus stage by an identification with the critical parent. This can apply to both boys and girls, depending in part on the bisexual disposition in children.

The term 'id' ('das Es' in German) is used in *The Ego and the Id* as a way of resolving the problems associated with the word unconscious for this word was being used as a descriptive term for a part of the mind which could 'contain' repressed wishes, and a term for a function of the mind which operated unconsciously. The 'id' is not the same, therefore, as the earlier term 'the unconscious' although in the second phase of his work Freud did tend to use 'the unconscious' as a synonym for the 'id'. The two are not the same because in the threefold model of id, ego, superego, the last two terms can be aspects of consciousness or unconsciousness. The unique contribution of psychoanalytic theory to the social sciences in general remains the distinction between the unconscious and consciousness, but now the understanding of the unconscious is richer with the introduction of the three concepts of ego, id, superego.

Psychoanalysis is concerned with the repressed material of the unconscious or id. This repressed material is not readily recallable into consciousness as is the case with ideas, or other psychical elements, which are merely outside the consciousness at a particular moment but which are readily brought into consciousness. This material which is easily remembered, but is temporarily out of the centre of attention, is the *preconscious*. The material in the preconscious is not being, and has not been, repressed as has that in the unconscious. This is why it is more easily remembered and brought to consciousness. No energy, or force, is in operation to keep it repressed as is the case with unconscious materials.

The 'id' is not just repressed material. It is the area from which internal feelings and desires emerge from the 'instincts'. This area is obscure, and difficult to describe. However, some notion such as this is required given the premisses of psychoanalysis developed by Freud up to this point.

The ego was once merged with the id. The ego develops as a result of contact with the external world, both physical and sociocultural, through sense perceptions and through the acquisition of language. Its roots remain in contact with the id. 'Moreover, the ego seeks to bring the influence of the external world to bear upon the id and its tendencies, and endeavours to substitute the reality principle for the pleasure principle which reigns unrestrictedly in the id.'[7]

The superego stands like a parent in relation to a child compelling the ego to obey. It derives this capacity to stand apart from the ego and to master it from the Oedipal situation — from the father. It is formed from object cathexes of the id, that is from the earliest attachments of the baby. As such it is in touch with the id and the phylogenetic archaic heritage of the id. This archaic heritage comes from the past of mankind, and Freud seems to think it is transmitted through heredity. This strikes people as a totally unscientific notion. It has been part of normal biology to assume that acquired characteristics cannot be transmitted by heredity. Whether this is still true is a matter for dispute within biology not within the psychoanalytic theory of 'the archaic heritage'. The best working assumption within psychoanalysis would be that the symbolism, values and emotions, of previous, very early, generations of mankind are transmitted through myths, folktales, nursery rhymes, religions, and that this is how children learn them. The manner of their acquisition would be different from that of intellectual learning, or rote learning. It would be by a process of unconscious learning that the archaic heritage is produced in children. This formulation would retain most if not all of the key components of Freud's theory without committing the error he did of making it seem as though a biological process was involved in the transmission of the archaic heritage. This will be discussed further in the next sections of this chapter.

The superego manifests itself in criticism of the ego, which results in the person feeling guilty. In therapeutic settings Freud found that some patients were unconscious of this guilt, so that it operated in them, or on them, in ways of which they were unaware. They would remain ill, or become ill again, just when the therapy seemed to be making good progress as a way of punishing themselves.

The superego uses energy from the death instincts to turn on the ego with its criticisms of the inadequacies of the person given the standards of the ego-ideal, both the positive ones of what the ego should be, and negative ones about what the ego should not do, and desire to do. The sadism which could be directed on to others in the external world is turned on the self in the criticisms of the superego. This produces a sense of guilt. Freud wrote in *The Ego and the Id:*

> How is it that the superego manifests itself essentially as a sense of guilt (or rather, as criticism — for the sense of guilt is the perception in the ego answering to this criticism) and moreover develops such extraordinary harshness and severity towards the ego? ... Following our view of sadism, we should say that the destructuve component had entrenched itself in the superego and turned against the ego. What is now holding sway in the superego is, as it were, a pure culture of the death instinct, and in fact it often enough succeeds in driving the ego into death, if the latter does not fend off its tyrant in time by the change round into mania.[8]

Guilt is destructive aggressiveness turned on the ego of a person instead of being discharged on external objects in the world. For this reason Freud shows that the person who is inhibited in expressing aggression towards external objects, such as parents, is all the more severe with themselves. This is because the superego can use this unused aggressivity and turn it on the ego of the person. So when someone inhibits an aggressive wish toward another, instead of feeling pleased with themselves for obeying the moral values associated with an ethic like the Christian one of love to all, including enemies, and of turning the other cheek, they experience dissatisfaction with themselves. The internal, unconscious, criticism of the ego by the superego is more severe because it has more destructive energy to use if this has not been discharged on the external world. The meek and mild become more and more miserable for they are burdened with guilt.

This aspect of Freudian theory overlaps with moral philosophy despite Freud's claims to be developing a science not a philosophy. This is something which is seen as a fault by those who hold that science and ethics should not meet or be mixed together. Freud seems to have held such a view about science himself. For others, such as critical theorists, this feature is a strength in Freudian theory and makes it part of a contributor to a wider critical theory of Western societies and cultures.

Freud's position, which is reached he would claim through careful clinical work and the rational development of theory in the light of this work and not through the method of non-scientific speculation, does have some considerable similarities with the moral philosophy of Nietzsche. Both of them developed a critical approach towards the ethic of Judeo — Christianity which was in some respects more radical than that developed by Marx. Marx still retained the ideals of justice for all, developed by the Greeks and by Christianity, but he included all men and women, unlike the Greeks who had excluded slaves, barbarians, and to some extent women, and removed Christian theology. Freud and Nietzsche are cynical about demands for equality and justice for all including the sick, the inferior, and the untalented when this is at the cost of the development of healthy and talented people.

So who are the healthy & talented?

RELIGION AND SOCIETY

Freud made a major, if controversial, contribution to the study of religion in human societies. At first sight this area may seem remote from clinical therapeutic work in psychoanalysis, so it is worth attempting to see why Freud became interested in religion and society. This interest was not just one he developed towards the end of his life, as is sometimes suggested, as though he were having second thoughts before his death. He had had an interest in the moral teachings of religious groups from the first ten years of his work in psychoanalysis, as was shown above in the discussion on morality with reference to the 1908 paper on 'Civilized sexual morality and modern nervous illness'.[9]

This paper helps a great deal in understanding why Freud became interested in religions because it deals with the effects the sexual morality of Orthodox Judaism and Roman Catholicism may have on some people. Freud thought that these moral standards were too demanding for most people and claimed that his clinical practice had shown that people became ill with emotional and hysterical physical symptoms as a result of having been socialized into accepting such a morality. Such people fell ill because they could not find satisfactory ways to handle the erotic desires which they had, but which they had learned from their religious and parental upbringing were sinful and wrong. They could not, they dare not, express them in actions and even suffered if they acknowledged that they did have such erotic feelings towards people they knew were forbidden to them as sexual partners. Nor could these patients find satisfactory ways to sublimate these forbidden desires by, for example, creating art or science. They could not do this either because they had not the talent, or it had not been developed in them. On the other hand, a man such as Leonardo da Vinci (1452-1519). a major Italian artist and scientist of the Renaissance, had fully expressed his potential. Freud tried to analyse how he had done so.

Leonardo da Vinci had been able to sublimate his erotic desires into his creative work. Freud had written a case study of Leonardo which had been published in 1910;[10] he was realistic enough to know that most people could never achieve this degree of creative sublimation. Nevertheless he had felt it was important to try to work out how artists and scientists could achieve great creative heights in order to deepen the theory of sublimation, and to see more clearly what it was many neurotics were not able to achieve psychically. Neurotics neither sublimated their forbidden erotic desires, as did artists and scientists for example, nor did they act on them in the way adults who indulged in perverse sexual acts, or who were homosexual or lesbian, did. Neurotics suffered with their symptoms which were produced by unexpressed erotic desires in those organs or processes of the body which were closely associated with their sexual desire.

Religious morality played a key role in these processes. As Freud developed his theory of religion it became clearer that changes in sexual moral teachings were not going to be as easy to achieve as he had thought they would be at the outset. This was because the moral teachings of the religions he looked at did not just have the negative consequences with which he was familiar from his patients, but had some positive consequences for the development of culture and for the more basic maintenance of any society as will be shown later. There were also strong irrational, non-utilitarian, forces at work in the maintenance of high standards of sexual morality. This made it very difficult, if not impossible, to achieve changes in morality through rational argument. This did not mean that changes in sexual morality should not be sought. Freud and others did try to argue for changes in attitudes towards the role of women and towards homosexuality, for example. However, it did sound a note of caution. Sex morality reformers should not be too disappointed if their ideas were opposed by some, especially by the officials in the religious institutions and in the laity.

In the period since Freud's death some societies in the West have experienced a degree of sexual liberation. Birth-control is widely available and used, even by some Roman Catholics who are still taught that sexual intercourse is primarily for procreation and not for pleasure. The Papal Encyclical *On Human Life,* which was produced in 1968, continued the traditional sexual teachings of the Church in the area of marriage and birth-control. So the change has not been all in one direction.

Some societies have changed their laws on male homosexuality, allowing two consenting males over a specific age, which varies from one society to another, to have erotic relationships without fear of being prosecuted for an illegal act. At the same time the number of prosecutions for male homosexuality outside these limits has risen in a country such as Britain. Religious groups are on the whole against teaching the young that homosexuality or lesbianism are paths for some if they wish to take them. They may even have heightened their vigilance as a result of being made aware of different sexual orientations, and be more concerned to condemn these practices in some cases. Some religious groups are actively in favour of accepting homosexuality and lesbianism; others are in favour of outlawing or morally condemning them. Most are in a state of confusion somewhere between these two positions.

There have, then, been some changes since Freud published his ideas, but they are not so great as to make his theory unimportant in the contemporary situation in Western societies, nor for others in other parts of the world, such as those societies influenced by Islam. It is, therefore, sociologically relevant to study Freudian theory of religion because the area of sexual morality, to take one particular but central concern, is still an area contested by traditional religionists and by secular rationalists.

Freud developed his theory of religion in a series of texts and papers produced throughout the forty years in which he was developing psychoanalysis. These texts, therefore, each reflect the stage of development of the wider theory of psychoanalysis at the time they were written. So *Totem and Taboo* (1912-13) reflects the theory of psychoanalysis at that stage of development, that is *before* the introduction of the death instincts in 1920. The other major texts concerned with religion, *Group Psychology and the Analysis of the Ego* (1921), *The Future of an Illusion* (1927), *Civilisation and its Discontents* (1930), *Moses and Monotheism* (1939), are all written after the introduction of the death instincts, and all but *Group Psychology* are written after the introduction of the id, ego, superego model of the mind.

Totem and Taboo [11] is concerned with themes which were preoccupying Freud around that time, 1910-12, namely Oedipus, the incest taboo, totemic symbols among primitives and among children in European societies, and emotional ambivalence. It is divided into four essays. The first deals with incest, 'The Horror of Incest'. It starts by Freud setting out his working assumption that the pre-literate peoples studied by social anthropologists can tell us something about prehistoric people's ways of thinking and acting. This assumption was made by Durkheim too in his study of aboriginal totemism. It is one which has since been challenged by anthropologists, for example Claude Lévi-Strauss in his books on *Totemism* (1962) and *La Pensée Sauvage* (1962) (*The Savage Mind*). Lévi-Strauss works on the assumption that the ways of thinking of the modern mind, as in binary computer language, and the ways of thinking of primitives are more similar than they are different. Classification into categories characterizes both kinds of thought and there is no superiority to be attached to modern scientific thinking compared with primitive classification.[12]

Freud assumes that there has been some progress in rational thinking which has been made by Western peoples, and shares with Max Weber an interest in this unique form of rationality. He does not assume that it is easily achieved or maintained by either individuals or in whole societies, but he does assume that there is a significant qualitative difference between primitive thought (la pensée sauvage) and rational thought. This is an important difference between Freud's starting point and that of French structuralists like Lévi-Strauss, or other relativists within social anthropology too numerous to discuss here.

There is nothing too objectionable about Freud's starting point if this point is kept in mind. He does go on to make other connections which are also capable of being misunderstood unless they are seen in the context of his assumption about the qualitative superiority of some forms of thinking and acting over others. Freud assumes that there are some similarities between all the following: prehistoric peoples, contemporary 'primitive' peoples, aspects of the thought and action of traditional, historical civilizations, children and modern neurotics! This can seem to be an extraordinary list of groups of people to link together unless it is seen in the context of Freud's assumption that some people think and behave more rationally than others. His list connects those groups which do not think or act in predominantly rational ways. For example, Freud is clear that magical practices typically have more in common with irrational, or non-rational, ways of thinking and acting than they do with modern thinking and actions based on science and technology. This would be clear in different beliefs about, and techniques for curing, various illnesses such as malaria, or yellow fever, or malnutrition. Freud assumes the Western forms of rationality in medicine and technology are superior to primitive methods of acting and thinking. He is not a relativist in such matters.

To return to the body of the text titled 'The Horror of Incest'. He begins by taking the Australian aborigines as an example of the most primitive peoples known to Europeans, exactly like Durkheim did at the same time, 1911–13. The aborigines do not build houses, as do Melanesian and Polynesian peoples, and many groups in Africa. They do not cultivate the soil; nor do they keep domesticated animals except the dog. They are not acquainted with the art of making pottery, nor clothing. They eat whatever they can find in the outback, and drink the scarcest resource of all, water, if and when they find it.

The social and cultural life of the aborigines contains no kings, nor high gods. It is communal and is organized around totemic emblems into clans. The totem is often an animal, bird or plant. Sometimes it is another natural but intangible object such as rain, or sky.

Aborigines show a deep horror of incest – they are by no means living without sexual morality in the way some Europeans imagined primitives lived. They may not marry someone from the same totemic clan as themselves – to do so would evoke the feelings of horror of breaking the taboo on such sexual relationships. (Members of different totemic clans may live and move around together, so a totem is not fixed to a settled dwelling place but to a group.) Freud quotes J. G. Frazer's *Totemism and Exogamy* (1910), 'In Australia the regular penalty for sexual intercourse with a person of a forbidden clan is death'.[13] The number of women with whom a man of say the Kangaroo clan may not have sex relations is larger than just those who are his sisters and his mother in the Western sense. The incest taboo affects *socially defined* relatives, not only physically related individuals. It is fundamental to morality and basic to the organization of human societies such as the most primitive form of Australian aborigines.

In the second section of *Totem and Taboo* Freud develops further his ideas of emotional ambivalence and taboo which he began in the first section. Taboos exist where there is a strong emotional desire to perform an act, usually a sexual act; they may take the form of prohibitions to do something. But 'taboo' as a term within Polynesia means something much broader, and is close to everything that is set apart from utilitarian use, rather like Durkheim's definition of the 'sacred'. Freud suggests the term 'holy dread' for taboo.[14] A taboo is unlike a moral prohibition in that no reasons are given for it. Freud discusses various definitions of taboo from anthropologists, stressing the automatic nature of the effects of breaking a taboo, or coming into contact with tabooed objects or persons.

There is a similarity between taboos and the obsessional prohibitions some neurotics develop, and Freud says it is worth following this up to see if psychoanalysis can throw any light on taboos. For example, in obsessional prohibitions on touching something there is usually a strong *ambivalence* – on the one hand there is a strong desire to touch the object, and on the other a strong sense of disgust about the object. These obsessional prohibitions in neurotics have their source in childhood experiences of the patient. Children are often told not to touch or play with their genitals, although they retain the desire to do so they may well give up infantile masturbation. Or some children may be told not to play with their faeces even though they have a strong desire to do so. Later they learn to feel disgust at the idea.

Taboo may be seen as surrounding acts which there is a strong desire to perform. Two basic ones are given as examples: the desire to eat the totem animal which is forbidden in totemism, and the desire to have sexual relations with members of the totem clan of the opposite sex. These acts are surrounded with emotional ambivalence. Freud wrote:

> ... one thing would certainly follow from the persistence of the taboo, namely that the original desire to do the prohibited thing must also persist among the tribes concerned. They must therefore have an ambivalent attitude towards their taboos. In their unconscious there is nothing they would like more than to violate them, but they are afraid to do so; they are afraid precisely because they would like to, and the fear is stronger than the desire. The desire is unconscious, however, in every individual member of the tribe just as it is in neurotics.[15]

People who break taboos themselves become taboo because they have done what others have a desire to do. People are unconscious of their desires in these areas and so experience no contradiction between treating the taboo breaker as contagious and their own unconscious desire to do the forbidden act. An example from Western societies could be the way some people still behave towards lesbians or male homosexuals – they still treat openly homosexual or lesbian persons as carrying a degree of stigma or taboo. Those who expend a great deal of energy attacking homosexuality are seen by those with a little psychoanalytic understanding as doing so *because* they have unconscious homosexual desires themselves.

Freud discusses three examples of taboo taken from Frazer's *The Golden Bough* (1911): the treatment of enemies; the treatment of priests, chiefs and rulers; and the taboo upon the dead. In each case Freud shows that there is a deep emotional ambivalence present — love and hate.

First the heads of enemies that have been killed are fed and spoken to like friends among the Sea Dyaks of Sarawak, the head having been brought to the hut after the decapitation. Similar behaviour is found among other groups such as American Indians like the Choctaw, where a warrior goes into mourning for a month after killing and scalping an enemy. Such behaviour shows some remorse, some admiration for the enemy, and a bad conscience for having killed him.

Secondly priestly kings are both feared and revered. Coming into contact with them often involved rituals which helped to protect the subject from the unearthly power of rulers. The touch of the sovereign was often powerful enough to heal illness. For example, as recently as the reigns of the English kings Charles I (1625–49) who claimed the divine right of kings to rule, and Charles II (1660–85), there were many instances of people seeking to be touched by the king to be healed. Freud sees such beliefs as irrational and quotes King William III (1689–1702) who only ever put his hands on an ill person once with the words: 'God give you better health and more sense'.[16] These practices continue, however, as when people seek healing from priests, faith healers, and the Pope.

People act to protect their rulers, religious leaders and chiefs from danger, but they also perform rituals and ceremonials to protect themselves from the power of these same figures. Such power is not always or necessarily positive and healing. It may be evil in its consequences. Priestly kings and rulers were often surrounded by very detailed taboos about the tasks of daily life, such as eating, hair-cutting, nail-clipping, and concerning when and where they could walk. These were seen as protecting the rulers, but also made their lives less enviable to others. They were an expression of the unconscious hostility felt by subjects to them, as well as appearing to be done for their protection from danger.

Thirdly, not only are dead bodies usually, if not universally, treated as taboo objects, but those in close relationship and contact with them are too. The name of the dead may not be spoken among many peoples all over the globe. People think that saying the name will bring the ghost of the dead back again. The dead spirits are often thought to be demons with evil intentions towards the living. These beliefs and practices surrounding mourning Freud sees as deriving from the ambivalence of the living towards the dead. The surviving people harboured unconscious wishes of hatred towards the dead person, especially if they have been dying for some time and required to be looked after by a relative. The wish that they would die is usually unexpressed and repressed. It *returns in a projected form* in the belief that the dead person now has evil intentions towards the living person.

Mourning rituals express both affection and love towards the dead, and handle the unconscious hostility too. Modern civilized people do not expend so much energy on handling these ambivalent feelings towards the dead. They manage to do their mourning and carry on living. Modern neurotics cannot do this — they cannot let go of the dead and cling on to them in various ways which prevent them enjoying their own lives. It is from his work with patients of this kind that Freud generated his psychoanalytic theory of emotional ambivalence which he used in his explanations of taboos. Primitives are therefore acting collectively in the same way as some neurotics do in modern societies in the ways in which they try to handle their emotional ambivalence of love and hate towards significant others. This is not to say that primitives are neurotics, but that their collectively shared cultural beliefs and rituals can be seen and understood as if they were collective neurotic solutions. Freud is clear elsewhere that *collectively* shared ritual action can precisely save an individual having to invent his own *private* neurotic obsessional rituals. Therefore primitive peoples are saved from having to become individually neurotic by their collective rituals and beliefs. Their cultures are to this extent forms of collective group therapy.

By extension it is possible for Freud to see some aspects of modern religions as performing similar therapeutic ends and saving their adherents from the need to invent their own private ritual system of the kind the obsessional neurotic has to develop. Primitive groups have then a collective form of therapy which has been retained in the archaic institutions of religions. They have less individual neurosis as a result of having a shared common culture which is largely lost in modern industrial capitalist and socialist societies. In these societies without a collective therapeutic culture individuals are forced to choose between a commitment to a particular non-rational religious framework, or worse, to become neurotic. However such neurotic illnesses can help in the understanding and explanation of primitive cultures' taboos which in turn helps further understanding of more recent religious beliefs and practices.

One difficulty Freud had in this period of his work was that he had not introduced the concept of the death instincts into psychoanalysis. Yet he is very much concerned in *Totem and Taboo* with wishes to see the death of someone, and even to murder. For instance, people subject to rulers in primitive societies often have unconscious wishes to murder their king, and may do so under circumstances when they feel the king has brought misfortune on them. The theory of emotional ambivalence includes two ideas: that there is a desire to have sexual relations with some object which is taboo for that reason, and that there is a wish to kill some people, who are then protected seemingly from others by elaborate rituals and taboos. Love and hate, that is to say these wishes to have sexual relations and to kill, exist in the unconscious side by side, but not as a mixed form. The mixed form may appear at the conscious level of social action as affection which is a fusion of love and hate. Freud makes these claims in part on the basis of dreams where such wishes may not be under so much disguise as they are in conscious living, and in part on what some extreme cases of perversion and murder in modern societies seem to show about unconscious wishes and desires which everyone has, but which they do not act out in real events.

In the third section of *Totem and Taboo,* which is called 'Animism, Magic and Omnipotence of Thoughts', Freud sketches out his psychoanalytic perspective towards the belief in spirits (animism) and the associated techniques of magic. His position is similar to that of Auguste Comte, the French founder of sociology, in that Freud also assumes three stages of development in human thinking in relation to the world, which he terms the animistic, the religious and the scientific. The animistic is distinguished from the religious by the feature which Freud makes central to his analysis, namely that in the animistic phase people ascribe omnipotence to *themselves,* and in the religious phase they transfer it to the gods, who can be influenced by men and women. 'The scientific view of the universe no longer affords any room for human omnipotence; men have acknowledged their smallness and submitted resignedly to death and to the other necessities of nature.'[17]

Animistic beliefs are based on wishes and on the power of wishes. They will not disappear because they persist among children in all societies, and among some people in more technologically developed societies. Freud again is assuming the technical and rational superiority of the scientific viewpoint, although aware that it is not widespread in those societies which have institutionalized technological scientific approaches to most problems. This comes out in one of the examples Freud uses from his main source Frazer:

At Norwich in June 1902 a woman named Matilda Henry accidentally ran a nail into her foot. Without examining the wound, or even removing her stocking she caused her daughter to grease the nail, saying that if this were done no harm would come of the hurt. A few days afterwards she died of lockjaw – as a result of this displaced antisepsis.[18]

In this part of the text one can find that one is at times bemused to find Freud connecting the thoughts and feelings of seemingly different groups — primitives, children, neurotics in modern societies and some examples from ordinary adults in the Europe of his own day, such as the woman quoted above. At first sight this sort of connection can appear absurd.

What is Freud trying to do? He is trying to say that some forms of belief are based on wishes; that is on an unconscious wish that something or other would happen. These wishes and fears of what might happen are very often of death — death of oneself or of another person. Neurotics may arrange complex obsessional ritual procedures for themselves which if not observed may cause their own, or someone elses, death. These kinds of belief systems are found among some *individuals* (neurotics), or among some special groups sharing the same cultural beliefs and magical practices (animism). Children also find satisfaction in their play activities in which they make believe that they are in a rocket going into space, or that they are running a home when playing with a doll's house, for example. In all these instances the emotional satisfactions are more important than the relation of the actions to reality. All share an assumption in 'the omnipotence of thoughts'; that is that manipulating ideas and feelings will make something happen, or prevent something happening, in reality. This is accepted without the need for reality-testing by the rational thoughts and practices of adults at the third stage of development in thinking, the scientific. Such adults may be found in pre-literate societies, but they are surrounded by many animistic beliefs and practices.

The final section of the text 'The Return of Totemism in Childhood' contains the important theory of *the primal horde*. It is introduced as a specifically psychoanalytic contribution to the explanation of religions in human societies, but as one of the factors, not the sole one. Religion, like other phenomena of interest to psychoanalysis such as dreams and neurotic symptoms, is *over-determined*, that is has two or more simultaneous determinants.

The social aspects of totemism had been examined in the first section of *Totem and Taboo* where Freud focussed on exogamy among the totemic clans and on the taboo on incest with members of the opposite sex of the same totem clan as the male. The ritual and religious aspects are of concern in the fourth and final section. The sacrifice of the totem animal in some rituals is to be explained, because ordinarily the totem animal may not be killed or eaten. The belief that a group is descended from the totem animal is associated with members of the totemic clan wearing the skin of the animal when this is possible for ritual dances, or with having a tatoo of it on their bodies. For example, the people indigenous to the island formerly called Ceylon, now Sri Lanka since independence, claim to be descended from the lion.

In much of Freud's writing he is using what Weberian sociologists would call an 'ideal-type' methodology. It is important to recognize that this is the case. Freud himself is not explicit about it in the way Weber was in his work. However, just as empiricist historians have often misunderstood Weber's method and treated it as simply empirical description, not as building up a conceptual model, as in the controversy over *The Protestant Ethic and the Spirit of Capitalism,* so empiricist anthropologists have sometimes misunderstood Freud on totemism. They have failed to see his work as theoretical, and his model of totemism as using Weber's ideal-type method, at least implicitly. He is trying to build up a conceptual model of totemism not to provide an empirical description of some example of it. This is done for theoretical purposes, but is not completely removed from concrete, empirical reality.

A major problem with the last section of *Totem and Taboo* is to work out the correct methodological status of the other model Freud developed – the primal horde and the actions within it. The notion of the primal horde is taken from Darwin and refers to the group that was the first group of *homo sapiens* as distinct from remaining as a group of that species's immediate predecessor. This makes Freud's starting point different from that of other people who have tried to explain totemism, including Durkheim's social explanation, and some psychological explanations that, for example, totemism began from the dreams of a single individual. Freud considers and rejects these approaches.

The psychoanalytic contribution begins with observations of the actions and talk of children. Children do not draw as hard and fast a line between themselves and animals as adults do; they notice they share a more matter of fact attitude towards bodily functions for instance. Some children develop an animal phobia, as Little Hans did towards horses for instance. This contrasts with their otherwise very positive attitude towards animals. The fear of a boy towards his father is projected onto an animal, and by a process of reversal the hatred towards father becomes a phobia that an animal will harm the child. The animal will be related to ambivalently – love and hate being felt at different times. An animal which has been one of the first a child meets and loves, such as a dog, or a cat, or horse, may later become the object of reversed hate, that is feared. (In the play *Equus* an adolescent boy worships horses; he rides them while nude and becomes so sexually excited that he ejaculates on the horse.) The Hindu reverence for the cow is totemic; to shed the blood of a cow is to attack the group.

If the totem animal is treated as a symbol for the father, the ancestor, then parallels with the Oedipus situation suggest themselves.

> The first consequence of our substitution is most remarkable. If the totem animal is the father, then the two principal ordinances of totemism, the two taboo prohibitions which constitute its core — not to kill the totem and not to have sexual relations with a woman of the same totem — coincide in their content with the two crimes of Oedipus, who killed his father and married his mother, as well as with two primal wishes of children, the insufficient repression or the re-awakening of which forms the nucleus of perhaps every psychoneurosis. If this equation is anything more than a misleading trick of chance, it must enable us to throw a light upon the origin of totemism in the inconceivably remote past. In other words, it would enable us to make it probable that the totemic system — like little Hans's animal phobia ... was a product of the conditions involved in the Oedipus complex.[19]

At the ritual sacrifice of the totem animal or bird and the eating of the flesh and blood of the slaughtered animal there is an enactment of the killing of the father — the father of the totemic clan. This is a symbolic killing of the father. Freud goes on to suggest that this symbolic version is one which started with the killing of the old male who had expelled his own sons from the group in which he lived with his females. In this primal horde situation there is domination by the old male over females, and over his expelled sons. This is the first patriarchal society. It produced parricide. The brothers banded together to kill their father. As Freud puts it: 'One day the brothers who had been driven out came together, killed and devoured their father and so made an end of the patriarchal horde. United, they had the courage to do and succeed in doing what would have been impossible for them individually'.[20]

This deed became the origin of the totem meal. It was the 'beginning of so many things — of social organization, of moral restrictions, and of religion'.[21] The sons, who had killed their father because they had hated him for keeping the women for himself and for being an obstacle to their desire for power and sexual satisfactions, loved and admired him too. The dead father became stronger than the living one had been as a result of the remorse and guilt the sons experienced. They forbade the killing of the totem animal, and repudiated sexual relations with the women, their mothers and sisters as a result of their guilt. This phenomenon Freud called 'deferred obedience'. Here are the unconscious sources of the incest taboo and of totemism; of morality, social organization, and religious rituals and symbols. It is worth connecting this analysis of totemism with the symbolism of the Lamb of God whose flesh and blood is symbolically imbibed in Christian ritual.

The incest taboo was set up not just out of deferred obedience but also to enable the brothers to continue to live cooperatively together. Sexual desire does not unite males but divides them in competition for women. The taboo on sexual relations with the women strengthened the group for other tasks. 'In this way they rescued the organization which had made them strong — and which may have been based on homosexual feelings and acts, originating perhaps during the period of their expulsion from the horde'.[22] Freud wrote:

> Features were thus brought into existence which continued thenceforward to have a determining influence on the nature of religion. Totemic religion arose from the filial sense of guilt, in an attempt to allay that feeling and to appease the father by deferred obedience to him. All later religions are seen to be attempts at solving the same problem. They vary according to the stage of civilization at which they arise and according to the methods which they adopt; but all have the same end in view and are reactions to the same great event with which civilization began and which since it occurred, has not allowed mankind a moment's rest.[23]

Further rebellions against the father, albeit in symbolic form can be seen in various religious movements which have developed over time. The developments of religions have been complicated by the fact that in totemic sacrifice the father appears twice; once as the sacrificial victim and again as the god to whom the sacrifice is made. The explanation of this double presence of the father is based on the unconscious feelings of ambivalence, of love and hate, towards him. He is hated and so killed; he is loved and so preserved as an invisible god.

New problems arose once rulers, kings, claimed to be God's representatives on earth, or to be gods in visible form again. Rebellion by the band of brothers starts again. Sacrifice became a human sacrifice of the kings who claim to be gods. Animal sacrifice preceded human sacrifice for there was no need to kill humans until the father symbolism had become too remote and returned to be represented by human beings.

The memory of the first human parricide became indestructible in human cultures, in their arts, religions and politics. The repressed returns time and time again in these spheres of social cultural action. The sons (and daughters in part) feel guilt for the parricide, and renewed rebelliousness at the restrictions placed on them by the will of the primal father transmitted in religious and state laws.

Youthful gods, such as Adonis, emerged in human religions who did break the incest rule by having sexual relations with mother, in the form of Mother Earth. Such mythic figures emerged with the introduction of agriculture, for tilling the soil is for psychoanalysis an expression of the unconscious desire to make love with mother.

Jesus, who was also a young man, a son, atoned for a sin of mankind by being sacrificed himself. This sin must have been a killing — the murder of the father. Jesus became himself the Son of God, and in the Christian communion meal it is the Son's flesh and blood that is devoured. But the Son is part of the Trinity; he is God too. The sacrifice of the Mass is a fresh elimination of the father too.

Freud ends the book by making it explicit that he is assuming that there is a collective unconscious mind which operates like the mind of individuals, and that Oedipal wishes are as central to the development of the cultures of mankind as they are to the individual. This is not an assumption with which he feels content, but at this stage there seems to be no other possible. Religions, myths, literature, morals, and social organizations of families, totemic clans or nations, are to be explained as overdetermined; explanations must be both historical and adequate in terms of what we know from psychoanalysis of the emotional lives of human beings. Freud claims to have begun such an explanation in *Totem and Taboo*. He developed it further in other writings on religions, morals and society which followed. These will be discussed before later critiques of Freud are presented and assessed in the final chapter.

GROUP PSYCHOLOGY

In *Group Psychology and the Analysis of the Ego* (1921)[24] Freud is concerned to further develop the analysis of human groups, using ideas developed in *Totem and Taboo* especially. He begins with a discussion of Le Bon's work on 'groups' or crowds ('foule' in LeBon; 'masse' is the German word used by Freud). Freud points out the similarity between LeBon's description of the crowd and the behaviour of children and primitives with his analysis in the third section of *Totem and Taboo*. People in crowds cannot tolerate delays in gratifying their desires. Crowds develop a sense of omnipotence; 'the notion of impossibility disappeared for the individual in a group' (i.e. in a crowd here). Crowds are influenced by feelings and images rather than by rational thought, or reality-tested ideas, so they can be described as irrational. Crowds are conservative, they have a deep aversion to innovations and advances, they respect and willingly obey the authority of the leader(s). A crowd 'wants to be ruled and oppressed and to fear its masters'.[25]

In a crowd individuals lose their inhibitions and are ready to give vent to their cruel, brutal, destructive instincts which lie dormant in people 'as relics of a primitive epoch'. People can also be stirred to carry out unselfish deeds by belonging to a crowd or group. Moral standards can be raised, or lowered, in crowds. Intellectual standards are always lowered. Crowds have no interest in truth. Crowds are fascinated by certain key words as though they were magical incantations — another feature in common between LeBon's crowds and Freud's primitives in *Totem and Taboo*. Crowds want their leaders to be fascinated by a set of ideas, a faith, an ideology, and to possess what LeBon calls 'prestige'. This can be attached to a person or a set of ideas or both. The concept has similarities to Max Weber's notion of 'charisma' — a leader with a gift of grace, who can convince followers of his extraordinary powers.[26]

LeBon's work was based on the historical descriptions of crowds during the French Revolution of 1789. He had other observations of crowd behaviour to add to the historical material, but the French Revolution was his starting point. That Revolution had set out to achieve rational aims, and had failed, setting up a reign of terror instead.

Since Freud and LeBon wrote, the rise of Facism and Nazism seemed to confirm their analyses of crowds and their role in political popular movements for a later generation. Wilhelm Reich and the Frankfurt School writers found Freud's theory of mass psychology of crowds and their relationship to leaders of great interest in trying to unravel the causes of Fascism and Nazism.

Freud goes on to try to see what light is thrown on groups and crowds by the concept of libido derived from his own psychoanalytic theory of the emotions. This means showing how sexuality can be redirected to form the basis of other social ties than that of sexual union, as has been understood since St. Paul. 'Charity' was praised by St Paul and this is love in its wider connotation. The Greek word *eros* used by Plato is the sexual love of the libido in psychoanalytic theory; the Greek word *agape* used by St Paul is brotherly love, charity, or in psychoanalytic terminology aim-inhibited libido. Freud proposed to stress the sexual connotations of libido rather than making concessions to the critics of psychoanalysis who claim that the theory stresses sexuality too much by using a word like *eros,* or 'love' (i.e. in German the word *Liebe*).

Moving on from crowds Freud considers two organized groups, which would be called complex organizations by modern sociologists, namely the church and the army. Why these two? Freud mentions that they both have some features in common. Firstly as a rule a person is not given a choice about joining such groups. This seems to be true of some kinds of churches and not others, and to be true of conscripted armies, not volunteer armed forces. Secondly leaving churches and armies is difficult if not impossible. Freud argues that they are held together by a degree of external force. Thirdly, they have a head who loves all the individuals equally – Christ in the Catholic Church and the Commander-in-chief in the army. It is odd that Freud does not mention here the visible vicar of Christ on earth, the Holy Father, the Pope, but he does say that the invisible Christ can be held to know and to care more about each individual than any human figure.

These groups also have strong emotional ties among the members as well as between each member and the head figure. This libidinal structure of an army, for instance, is best seen by looking at a situation where it is absent. In the example of a panic in an army when the mutual ties between soldiers and officers break down, soldiers do not follow orders but look after themselves as individuals, or small groups of comrades outside the army.

In the Church there is a strong bond between members but cruelty, hostility and intolerance towards those who do not belong to it are natural to every religion. It is worth noticing at this point that because Freud has made Christ the head of the Church rather than priests, bishops, and the Pope, he cannot satisfactorily explain the mutual hatred of Christians for those belonging to one or other of the main streams of Christianity, especially Roman Catholicism and Protestantism. If he had used the Pope as the head of the Catholic Church his theory would have held up as a plausible explanation of these differences in a way that it does not do if all are related to Christ as the invisible head.

Socialism, and even scientific differences, are capable of producing the same kind of feelings of intolerance and hostility to outsiders that religions have generated in the past, Freud asserts. He does not follow up these examples here, but the point should be noted for it is important for assessing Freud's relation to socialism, and for his own view of the nature of the splits within psychoanalysis. By 1921 Jung and Adler had broken with Freud and he thought his position was more scientific than theirs, and that they were motivated by unconscious emotional factors towards himself as head of the psychoanalytic movement. There is an implicit agenda here which Freud leaves undiscussed — quite rightly in the context of a theoretical piece of work which is not a polemic, nor a piece of political ammunition within psychoanalysis.

Any group which lasts for some time, such as a family, or a work group, or a friendship between two or more people, generates feelings of aversion and hostility among its members. These feelings are very often repressed although they may be expressed in some situations. Likewise relations between groups generate hostile feelings, some of which may be expressed directly. Others repressed for most of the time may erupt explosively given the chance. Two towns may be rivals or two regions may be. Two closely juxtaposed countries may be hostile to one another like the dislike of the English for the Scot, or the Spaniard for the Portuguese. Wider differences lead to almost insuperable repugnance, such as the Aryan people feel for the Semite, and the white races for the coloured. In a footnote Freud points out that he has introduced the notion of death instincts in *Beyond the Pleasure Principle*, and that the basic deep-rooted hostility to others outside the group may derive from these instincts.

The analysis of the ego mentioned in the title of the 1921 text being considered here concerns the attempt to understand the processes involved in identification, being in love and in hypnosis. Freud thought that this would shed some further light on processes in groups, especially the emotional ties between group members, and between the leader(s) and members.

A small boy may identify with his father, that is he wants to become like him. He may take a more passive attitude and want to have the father take him as an object of love, in place of, or in addition to mother. A little girl may identify with her mother and want to become like her; or she may identify with her father, as Dora did in imitating her father's cough in one of Freud's previously published case histories. Dora had regressed from object-choice of her father to identification with him; 'regressed' because this is the first, earliest, form of emotional tie between a baby and another person.

'Being in love' means taking another person as an object for the sexual instincts. If these instincts are inhibited in their aim, that is do not lead to direct sexual acts, then a relation of affection is established as happens between parents and children, or between friends. Hypnosis functions on the basis of the hypnotized person being devoted to the hypnotist as a lover is to the object of their love, but with the possibility of sensual relations removed.

A group is formed on the basis of each member relating to the leader in a similar way to the situation in hypnosis — devotion to the leader by the members but with no sensuality — and with ties of aim-inhibited affection between the members. Sensual love is less long-lasting than affectional ties, unless the sensuality is part of a wider relationship which includes aim-inhibited bonds. A primary group which has not become an organized group like a rational bureaucracy, will be made up of a number of individuals who have put the same individual leader 'in place of their ego-ideal and have consequently identified themselves with one another in their ego'.[27] This definition of a primary group differs from others in social psychology in that Freud stresses the role of a leader as central to the unconscious structure of the group whereas other definitions do not emphasize leaders but rather peer groups with no clear leader. Teenage gangs are usually, but not always, structured around a leader; religious groups are typically structured around both an invisible figure and usually a visible leader on earth. Political groups need a leader who represents to others the ideals and beliefs of the particular ideology of the movement. On the other hand, groups of friends, and some families, may have no one person who is always seen as the leader. Such leaderless groups are usually called 'primary groups'.

Freud discusses whether there is a herd instinct in human beings alongside the instincts of sex, and self-preservation. He does not mention his newly formulated notion of the death instincts here. The herd instinct idea can be found to underlie Aristotle's notion of man as the 'political animal' — an idea developed by Marxists in their assumptions about mankind's essentially social and cooperative potentialities. Freud argues that such ideas as this underestimate the role of leaders in human groups. Humans are really horde animals, and belong in groups structured around leaders, not herd animals with no hierarchy.[28]

To the objection that people do feel a sense of community, a group of equals, as in peer groups without leaders, Freud points to the origins of these feelings in *envy*. Envy is an emotion of hostility towards others for they have something or someone desired by the person who feels envious and cannot attain it. It leads to demands for equality among groups. 'No one must want to put himself forward, every one must be the same and have the same. Social justice means that we deny ourselves many things so that others may have to do without them as well ... This demand for equality is the root of social conscience and the sense of duty.'[29] Equality is to apply to all except the leader who is to be superior to all members — that is the group formation which is most desired by most people and which is most stable according to Freud.

Freud is arguing, therefore, that there is a collective unconscious desire to arrange social groups, and societies into this type of group structure. People are all to be equal, but they will only know that they are equal if there is one superior leader above them, who can be loved and hated. This group structure which lurks behind all human societies is *the primal horde,* the concept Freud had first developed from Darwin in *Totem and Taboo* (1912).

Like all recoveries of unconscious desires this one is met with rejection by many people first of all. Unconscious desires have often to come into consciousness first of all by being denied, by the process called *negation* in a paper with the title 'Negation' (1925).[30] This is one way in which unconscious repressed desires are acceptable to the censor, the superego. However, these ideas belong to a later period of Freud's work. In *Group Psychology* they are present as embryonic ideas only.

The notion of the primal horde in *Totem and Taboo* was first criticized by anthropologists in America and England for being a 'Just-so-Story'. Freud agreed that it was a hypothesis, not proven fact, but a hypothesis which is able to bring coherence and understanding into more and more regions of research in analysis.

Just as there is a primitive layer in each individual, so there is a relic of the primal horde in any collection of individuals who form a group. Group psychology is the oldest form of psychology Freud asserts, by which he means that the primal horde is fundamental to human societies and their development in human evolution. The chief or leader of the primal horde was the first individual to emerge. This leader was first the primal father and this aspect persists in giving all leaders an air of the 'uncanny' — what Weberian sociologists would call 'charisma'. This type of legitimacy was the basic form for Weber in his work on authority and power, and is also the fundamental type in Freud's analysis even though his theory differs substantially from he calls it of the primal horde and the primal father introduced in *Totem and Taboo*. What is not clear in what Freud writes is whether he thinks human beings can collectively move beyond the primal horde with a leader for long periods of time, or whether societies which claim to be democracies with no leaders are deluded. They either will not survive for very long periods of time, or will develop a primal horde structure. For example, some societies have indeed set up dictatorial leaders over and above an equalitarian ethos among the remaining citizens.

When Freud was writing *Totem and Taboo* there had been no First World War, no Russian Revolution, no Fascist dictator in power. By the time he came to write *Group Psychology* in 1920-21 the First World War was over, Lenin had three more years as leader in Russia before Stalin was to take over, and the Italian Fascists led by Mussolini were a year or so away from power and the 'march on Rome' which occurred in 1922. Hitler was a relatively unknown figure, although he had formed the National Socialist German Workers Party in 1920. However, Freud was in touch with the roots of dictatorial stirrings in Europe. Vienna had Karl Lueger as its mayor from 1896-1910. He became leader of the German National Socialist Party in 1918. Lueger had inspired the young Adolf Hitler who used to sell the party paper in the streets of Vienna before the First World War. Lenin had been in Vienna before the 1917 Revolution. So although Freud was not involved actively in politics, he lived in a city which contained many who were active and in touch with the changes sweeping Europe during and after the Great War (1914-18).

His work on group psychology and on the primal horde would have little interest to later writers, such as the critical theorists, had European history developed differently from the way it did. Given that both communist and Fascist dictatorships did arise, Freud's theory has held the attention of serious social theorists ever since. The same is really true of Freud's last major text *Moses and Monotheism* which as will be seen below contains ideas which appear strange and unworthy of scholarly attention until it is realized that it comes close to anticipating societies it might be, does nevertheless exist as a superior form of thought and action than other non-rational ways, such as magic or irrational political movements, is a central part of Freud's overall position. So too is his assumption about humans being horde animals, and not a herd species. People are certainly social beings, but that does not lead Freud to assume that their sociality is always benign in its influences on people.

Freud developed the social theory within psychoanalysis in three main texts in the last twelve or more years of his life. These three — *The Future of an Illusion; Civilization and its Discontents; Moses and Monotheism* — are outlined and discussed in the next sections of this chapter. The methodological assumptions behind this aspect of psychoanalysis, as well as other sections of it, will be discussed in the final chapter.

THE FUTURE OF AN ILLUSION (1927)

In *The Future of an Illusion* [31] Freud distinguishes two central features of culture or civilization (he does not distinguish these two terms). The two features are on the one hand the knowledge and techniques to control and develop the forces of nature and to extract wealth from it to fulfil human needs, and on the other hand the regulations which adjust the relations of men to one another and especially the distribution of the available wealth. This starting point is not incompatible with Marxism, as Freudian–Marxists have seen. Both Freud and Marx start from the material relations of people with nature and with one another in their analyses of society.

Freud assumes that people are not 'spontaneously fond of work' and some degree of coercion is necessary to get the work a society needs doing done — although the coercion can take different forms from physical threats of punishment, to not having enough to eat, to money. Freud also assumes that people are more motivated to do what they do in societies and as individuals by their emotions than by reason. This has to be understood as a descriptive proposition, about

Freud assumes in this text, and in his other writings in social theory, that people are often hostile to civilization because it makes too great a set of demands on them for instinctual renunciation. Many people find that there are not enough direct instinctual satisfactions from building and maintaining civilization to make it worthwhile, and so are hostile to civilization:

> One would think that a re-ordering of human relations should be possible, which would remove the sources of dissatisfaction with civilization by renouncing coercion and the suppression of the instincts, so that, undisturbed by internal discord, men might devote themselves to the acquisition of wealth and its enjoyment. That would be the golden age, but it is questionable if such a state of affairs can be realized. It seems rather that every civilization must be built up on coercion and renunciation of instinct; it does not even seem certain that if coercion were to cease the majority of human beings would be prepared to undertake to perform the work necessary for acquiring new wealth. One has, I think, to reckon with the fact that there are present in all men destructive, and therefore anti-social and anti-cultural, trends and that in a great number of people these are strong enough to determine their behaviour in human society.[32]

There are some compensations available for the renunciation of desires such as incestous wishes, cannibilistic wishes, and wishes to kill. These compensations are: some protection from nature; the material wealth made possible by working together in a society; and also cultural compensations in ideologies such as nationalism which provides a feeling of superiority even to those who are exploited in a society which is dominant over others, such as Rome was, and some European nations were in Freud's lifetime. The arts provide cultural compensation to those who can find the spare time to cultivate them. Many forbidden and repressed wishes and desires find some form of sublimated expression in various art forms which can be satisfying to are found in most world religions: 'thou shalt not kill'; 'thou shalt not commit adultery'; and in Christianity 'love thy neighbour' and 'love your enemies'. Religion offers compensations to people by teaching that there is a higher part of mankind, the soul, which does not die. Although the body may suffer here on earth, the soul will continue to live in one form or another depending on the religious belief system. Even Buddhism assumes that the soul can be reincarnated even though it aims at what Western atheism takes for granted, namely the total extinction of the soul.

These moral values and beliefs are transmitted to individuals over the generations by the institutions of a society. Here Freud presents a perfectly acceptable picture of the process of cultural transmission of symbols and values with none of the complications associated with the idea of a genetic inheritance of past generations' experiences which can be found in his other writings sometimes.

The way a person responds to religion as he or she grows up will be affected by the person's relation to their parents, especially their father. He is a figure who is loved and admired for offering protection to the child, but is also hated and dreaded for saying 'No' to some of the child's desires. These feelings are found in a person's relations with the God or gods in the religion of their culture: love and hate. Atheism can be as much part of this process as is belief – for vehemently rejecting religion can be a release for hostile wishes towards the father. Freud does not make this point as explicit as this, but it follows from his position. He does make the point again that the use of reason is a possibility in this area as in others; that is, religious beliefs can be examined *rationally* for their truth or falsity. It is not possible to say that religion is above reason. If, as is sometimes said, religious beliefs are outside the field of rational appraisal – that they should be believed because they are profound but irrational – then the question arises which absurd beliefs to accept?

Religious ideas are not based on experience and reason. 'They are illusions, fulfilments of the oldest, strongest and most urgent wishes of mankind. The secret of their strength lies in the strength of those wishes.'[33]

These wishes are for the continuation of the protection offered the child by their father by a divine Providence; the demand for justice and the establishment of a moral order in which this demand is fulfilled; and the prolongation of earthly life so that these demands and wishes can be fulfilled, for they have not been in any civilization on the earth. These are the core illusions of religion according to Freud. They are not necessarily false or immoral ideas – but they are based on wishes. An illusion is defined as a belief motivated by the desire to see wishes fulfilled. Delusions are also motivated in the same way in some psychiatric patients, but a delusion is in clear contradiction with reality. It is a matter of judgement whether one calls religious beliefs illusions or delusions. For example, the idea that a Messiah will come and set up a golden age on earth is a delusion, Freud thought.

Freud argues that modern civilization runs greater risks in maintaining its religious institutions, beliefs and rituals, than in becoming critical of them. The educated have increasingly come to accept science rather than religion says Freud. The uneducated masses cannot be kept in ignorance of these changes for much longer. They have justifiable reasons for being hostile to a civilization their work makes possible but which they do not enjoy for lack of money, time, and education. If the only reason for not killing your neighbour is that it is against God's commandments what happens when the masses realize there is no God to give such commands?

Freud makes no mention of contemporary political movements here, although he does discuss communism elsewhere. Fascism was growing rapidly at the time Freud was writing, but Hitler did not take power in Germany until the election of 1933. Christianity has been revived recently in many people's eyes because the secular alternatives, Fascism and communism, seemed or seem to be so horrific. Freud's ideas are still very relevant for the sociological analysis of the changing fortunes of religious beliefs and their role in societies with different political and economic structures.

Freud held that there was a rational argument for the prohibition not to kill along the lines that if everyone was free to kill those they hated social life would become impossible. The issue here is not whether this is a good argument in ethics, but with why societies in the West still try to rest their morality on the illusion that moral values are God's will. Freud was very aware that the most advanced society technologically, namely the United States, was also the one which was most keen on being a Christian country. This is still true in the last half of the twentieth century as it was in the first half when Freud was writing. Britain is also formally a Christian society with an established church which is unused by most of the population much of the time, unlike the United States situation where more people go to church.

His analysis of religion as based on strong wishes does highlight the key factor that religions persist in societies because of their appeal to emotions, conscious and unconscious, and not because of reason. Sociologists have sometimes forgotten this point, especially when they assume that modern societies are, or ought to be, secular because they contain the institution of science and technology. This overlooks the point Freud makes central to his analysis: that religion feeds on emotions and can co-exist in the same individual with a scientifically educated mind, and certainly can exist in a whole society alongside science and technological achievements. As Freud had pointed out in his work on groups and crowds, people in a group or crowd are non-rational and are swayed by appeals to their feelings rather than by rational arguments. This does not rule out rational argument in science, or even in politics for a very few. But the primal horde haunts group psychology.

Is there not an inconsistency in Freud's position? He considers that there might be. An imaginary opponent of Freud's view is used in the text to voice the opinion that there is a contradiction between saying that people are largely governed by their passions and the recommendation that religion should be done away and morals based on reason. Freud replies by saying that there is no real contradiction in his position. People are relatively weak intellectually as adults, more feeble than they were as children when they possessed 'a radiant intelligence'. It is the socialization process which stunts their intellectual development.

Children have their sexual researches stopped in infancy, and this is especially so for many girls. They may often also be told stories about how babies are born, such as the one that the stork brings them. Added to this is a second set of untruths derived from religion. Children are therefore nearly always doubly stunted in their use of their own intellectual powers and taught early emotional methods of repression of sexual instincts, not rational methods of instinctual renunciation, and introduced to the collective neurosis of religion by adults. They are predisposed to follow their emotions as adults, rather than their reason, for this has been what they have been taught to do as infants and children.

'Men cannot remain children forever; they must in the end go out into "hostile life". We may call this "education to reality".' It is better not to introduce children to the 'bitter–sweet poison' of religion in childhood to see if this produces adults who are more capable of facing the reality of 'their insignificance in the machinery of the universe'. [34] And men are not without assistance in dealing with nature for they have developed science.

Freud's opponent then charges him with having illusions now: that men and women can create a more rational and tolerable existence on earth. He replies that his hopes are not delusions like those of religion; they can be proved to be mistaken once they have been tested in reality. Religion is like a childhood neurosis developed during and after the Oedipus phase. As such it is quite likely that humanity, at least in

Europe, could soon be ready to move beyond it just as young adults often grow out of their own childhood neuroses. If it does not happen of its own accord, then psychoanalytic therapy can aid adults overcome some if not all of their individual neuroses. It is possible that although people are very heavily influenced by their emotions their reason can become stronger in collective matters. 'The voice of the intellect is a soft one, but it does not rest until it has gained a hearing. Finally, after a countless succession of rebuffs, it succeeds. This is one of the few points in which one may be optimistic about the future of mankind, but it is in itself a point of no small importance.'[35] Freud concludes by saying: 'No, our science is no illusion. But an illusion it would be to suppose that what science cannot give us we can get elsewhere'.[36]

CIVILIZATION AND ITS DISCONTENTS (1930)

Civilization and its Discontents [37] is the central text of Freudian social theory. It tries to develop a theory about why people so often experience a sense of discontentment with their lives in civilized society, so much so that they will try to return to more primitive conditions which they think are less frustrating, or they will even contemplate pulling civilization apart. Indeed sometimes this does happen in fact. Again the historical context of this text should be noted — it was written before Nazism came to power in Germany, but after the First World War and the Russian Revolution of 1917.

The text uses all the major concepts of psychoanalytic theory to evolve and develop a social theory which can account for this phenomenon of discontent with civilized life. It makes use of the second version of the dual instinct theory: sexual and death instincts. It uses the notion of the superego developed in 1923 and draws on the analysis of religions made in *Totem and Taboo* and in *The Future of an Illusion*. It continues with the tension between reason and the passions which Freud saw as so fundamental and with the assumption that many strong emotions and desires are unconscious. There is a tension between the pleasure principle which the unconscious uses in its workings and the reality principle which the rational part of the ego uses in its dealings with the world and other people.

Human societies have developed religions, science and arts to help with the many pains, disappointments, and impossible tasks of life. The majority of people have religion only — neither science nor art — as a compensation. Increasingly people benefit from science and modern medicine and technology who do not themselves understand the theories of science. An educated minority have science and art and can, therefore, do without religion according to Freud.

Freud exaggerated the tensions between religion and science and arts. Many scientists have been and still are religious; and much art was religious in original inspiration, and sometimes is in modern works. However, it is true that some people do live without religion and this Freud sees as a great step forward for the individual as long as they can avoid needing their own personal neurosis to replace the collective one. It is also part of the process of humanity generally becoming more rational; first a minority then more and more people live this way.

Human beings aim at happiness, pleasure, and to reduce pain. They employ a variety of methods to achieve these goals apart from the three just mentioned, such as using drugs of one form or another, or making love relations central to their lives. A few may make professional work their central interest, and if this is freely chosen it may well use up most of the person's sexual and aggressive wishes in ways which are rewarded by society in terms of status and wealth.

There is no *one* way for everyone to follow because each person is constitutionally different with regard to their capacity to sublimate or repress desires without ill effects, and they will have learned to need different activities during their socialization. Religions make the key mistake of supposing that there is one pattern which everyone should follow. People develop their own patterns, with little help from others, unless they go into therapy to help them work out a pattern of living suitable for them.

The major source of pleasure most people pursue is love; a few may pursue aim-inhibited love all their lives; but the majority seek sexual pleasures within a relationship. Human beings are faced with a dilemma, however. This is that there is a tension between the needs of building and maintaining culture and civilization which requires restrictions on sexuality in order that there be some surplus libidinal energy available for sublimation, and the desires of lovers to be left alone. This is one of the assumptions Freud makes about the reasons for the restrictions on the sexual instincts which civilization makes.

It has, of course, been challenged, with some writers pointing out that many artists for instance have been highly creative and have been very sexual too. If this is possible with artists then it cannot be the case that culture is created at the expense of libidinal energy. This may have been the case for Leonardo da Vinci, or Michelangelo, two artists Freud studied, but was not the case with J. S. Bach, nor Wagner. It might seem that it is homosexual libido which men sublimate into art, because this is forbidden in this culture, whereas heterosexual desire is socially approved within marriage at least. The ancient Greek artists however lived in a society in which the taboo on male homosexuality did not exist in the form that it did in Christian Europe. They nevertheless created art, science and philosophy.

Women, Freud argues, are often antagonistic to culture and civilization because men who engage in art, or science, political life or business, withdraw time and energy from sexual and family life at home. Women, however, did initiate the start of civilization by setting up the family as a social institution for child care and rearing. This may have been among women themselves first of all, a kind of mutual aid society, with the men having to be the protectors and hunters of the group of women and children. The nuclear family has arisen later, out of early stages of the development of culture as in totemism. Freud is not therefore maintaining that women are biologically opposed to civilization, but that they are hostile to it for social and cultural reasons. They are primary carers of children. Freud's analysis of the role of women would fit rural women more than bourgeois women in capitalist cities. This later group of women have been the mainstay of theatres, concerts, art galleries, libraries and bookshops − but Freud would point out no doubt that they were more often the audiences than the artists. Similarly in business and political life, women are often key supporters of politicians and businessmen, without many of them being able to break into these spheres as much as men have been able to.

Freud writes in a way which is sometimes ambiguous in this text. It is not as clear as it needs to be that there is an *analysis* of the role of women contained in the book, and not an apology for the male domination found in Western civilization. The two are capable of being distinguished. Freud intends his work to be treated as scientific analysis, but it sometimes affects readers as an apology for male domination. This can be seen as a problem caused both by some readers unfamiliarity with psychoanalysis and with Freud's own way of writing. Some readers do not see the analysis because they are overwhelmed by their feelings about the situation being described. Freud was not fully in control of his feelings towards women and the feminists in his own day, especially in the last ten years or so of his life. His anti-feminist prejudices do show through in the writings of his later years more than they should.

Turning back now to the social theory which is the central concern in *Civilization and its Discontents.* There is another reason for civilization's restrictions on sexuality apart from the one just discussed about the need for sublimation of sexual energy into producing all aspects of culture and civilization, from technology for work on nature to create food and shelter to science, art and politics. This is that because people are mutually hostile and antagonistic towards one another surplus libidinal energy is needed for work groups and family groups to sustain themselves over long periods of time. The destructive aggressive wishes, which derive from the death instincts in this stage of psychoanalytic theory, cannot be expressed directly in most social groups if they are to continue and to carry out their tasks satisfactorily. Freud wrote:

> In consequence of this primary mutual hostility of human beings, civilized society is perpetually threatened with disintegration. The interest of work in common would not hold it together; instinctual passions are stronger than reasonable interests. Civilization has to use its utmost in order to set limits to man's aggressive instincts and to hold the manifestations of them in check by physical reaction-formations. Hence, therefore, the use of methods intended to incite people into identifications and aim-inhibited relationships of love, hence the restriction upon sexual life, and hence too the ideal's commandment to love one's neighbour as oneself — a commandment which is really justified by the fact that nothing else runs so strongly counter to the original nature of man.[38]

Freud argues that the communists are mistaken in assuming that this aggressiveness will disappear when private property is abolished throughout one society, or in the world as a whole. This may be worth doing for reasons of economic equality and to abolish poverty — that is matter for political economic judgement. But it will not eliminate aggressiveness. 'Aggressiveness was not created by property. It reigned almost without limit in primitive times, when property was still very scanty, and it already shows itself in the nursery almost before property has given up its primal anal form ...'[39] To abolish property would deprive humanity of one of its ways of coping with aggressiveness. Possessing more than someone else may have some bad consequences, but it is not as bad as killing or torturing. Communism is based on an untenable illusion about the sources of human destructiveness. Freud argues:

> ... the dream of a Germanic world-dominion called for antisemitism as its complement; and it is intelligible that the attempt to establish a new, communist civilization in Russia should find its psychological support in the persecution of the bourgeois. One only wonders, with concern, what the Soviets will do after they have wiped out their bourgeois.
>
> If civilization imposes such great sacrifices not only on man's sexuality but on his aggressivity, we can understand better why it is hard for him to be happy in that civilization.

In fact, primitive man was better off in knowing no restriction of instinct. To counterbalance this, his prospects of enjoying this happiness for any length of time were very slender. Civilized man has exchanged a portion of his possibilities of happiness for a portion of security.[40]

Human aggressiveness opposes the work of Eros to unite human beings into larger and larger groups, and to create a united world of peace among nations and peoples. In the individual this destructive aggression is turned against the ego in the work of the superego. This results in the experiences of guilt in those with a severe superego; and in milder forms of discontent in others. Here the death instincts' energy is turned on the self. But this is an unstable form among many people, for there is less discontent if the destructive impulses can be expressed onto outer objects – other people, or nature, or man-made objects.

The superego does not distinguish between a deed and a wish in the unconscious. This means that a person with a strong superego will feel guilty for every wish, sexual or aggressive, which may not lead to an action at all. So even the virtuous, or perhaps one should say especially the virtuous, experience guilt for deeds they have not committed.

The situation is even stranger from the point of view of psycho-analysis. Every wish to be aggressive towards someone which is re-nounced feeds the strength of the superego. The person feels more guilty as a result of not acting in an aggressive and angry way because the aggression is turned on the self by the criticism of the superego. These processes are typically unconscious, and one of the greatest benefits Freud thought psychotherapy could aim to provide for the over-virtuous person was a reduction in the severity of the superego. The therapist is less critical of the sexual and aggressive wishes of the analysand. In so far as the therapist is internalized in place of the existing ego-ideal, which is based on past identifications with other people, then the analysand comes to feel less guilty. The meaning of the following proposition of Freud should now be clearer: '... the price we pay for our advance in civilization is a loss of happiness through the heightening of the sense of guilt'.[41]

Religions have never overlooked the part played in civilization by the sense of guilt. In Christianity the claim to redeem mankind from this sense of guilt, which is called sin in religious terminology, by the death of a single person is presented. The sense of guilt persists, how-ever. It cannot be erased so easily because of the persistence of the desire to kill the father – both the father figure in the individual's life and the primal father. The primal father was killed in the primal horde and this produced remorse in the sons who did the murder. Freud calls this remorse, not guilt, because the deed was carried out. Guilt is set up in children and continues in adults because the desire to kill persists, even if the deed is not carried out.

Religious institutions represent the cultural superego to successive generations. The cultural superego is influenced by specific leaders, such as Jesus Christ, who take on characteristics of the primal father after death. The cultural superego can be over-severe as can the superego in the individual. Freud wrote:

> It, too, does not trouble itself enough about the facts of the mental constitution of human beings. It issues a command and does not ask whether it is possible for people to obey it. On the contrary, it assumes that a man's ego is psychologically capable of anything that is required of it, that his ego has unlimited mastery over his id. This is a mistake; and even in what are known as normal people the id cannot be controlled beyond certain limits. If more is demanded of a man, a revolt will be produced in him or a neurosis, or he will be made unhappy. The commandment, 'Love thy neighbour as thyself', is the strongest defence against human aggressiveness and an excellent example of the unpsychological proceedings of the cultural superego. The commandment is impossible to fulfil; such an enormous inflation of love can only lower its value, not get rid of the difficulty. Civilization pays no attention to all this; it merely admonishes us that the harder it is to obey the precept the more meritorious it is to do so.[42]

Freud returned to these issues in *Moses and Monotheism*.

MOSES AND MONOTHEISM (1939)

The first two chapters of this text had appeared in the journal *Imago* in 1937 and 1938. Other parts of the book, which includes two prefaces at the beginning of Chapter 3, were written later during the period of uncertainty in Vienna before and after the Nazis' move into Austria in March 1938. Freud had hesitated to publish the book in Austria because he did not wish to upset the Catholic Church which was the only major non-Nazi institution functioning after the entry of Hitler into Vienna.

Once in London Freud no longer had any reason to withold publication.[43] The text is muddled in its construction as a result of the circumstances in which it was written. It is better treated as metaphor than as a contribution to history.

The major issue discussed in the book which is of interest to sociologists and social theorists concerns Freud's analysis of the relations of Judaism and Christiantiy in Europe, and of the Jews and the Germans in particular. He maintains that the problem of anti-semitism is not like that of other forms of hostility between ethnic and religious groups of different traditions, such as that between Hindus and Muslims in India. There is something specific about anti-semitism which has unconscious roots of a unique kind. To understand what these are it is necessary to follow Freud's arguments about the origins of Judaism. Judaism is the most monotheistic religion. There is only one God, not many gods, goddesses, or saints.

Judaism is the result of a long process of development in which the figure of Moses is central. Freud argues that there were in fact two men called Moses. One was an Egyptian — the word for child in ancient Egyptian was *mose*. This Moses, Freud asserted, introduced circumcision to the Jews as a mark of holiness. Freud maintained that circumcision was an Egyptian rite. This is a disputed point among scholars. The other Moses was a Midianite who introduced the Jews to the local volcanic god, Yahweh. Judaism is a fusion of the ancient Egyptian god Aten — the one invisible, loving God — and of Yahweh, who was bloodthirsty and harsh in his dealings with humans. The Jews killed the Egyptian Moses, but refused to acknowledge that they had done so. This killing of a father figure was a traumatic event which continued to influence the Jews unconsciously.

The Jews produced an attempt to handle this repressed memory by developing Christianity, which was originally a sect within Judaism. In this religious development a Son was offered to the Father to assuage the guilt for the earlier parricide — the murder of the Egyptian Moses. Later this was to be turned against them, as in the Middle Ages in Europe when the Jews were accused of having murdered the founder of Christianity. The Jews were subjected to pogroms in this period of European history. Freud was writing before the Nazis introduced the Final Solution to the problem of the Jews in Europe. However, he was aware of the hatred of the Germans for the Jews as this developed under Nazism. The Germans were relatively late in being converted to Christianity, and they hated the new religion. They desired to return to a more pagan, less instinctually restrictive creed. Freud argued that the German National-Socialist hatred for the Jews was at root a hatred of Christianity. Christianity was seen as a Jewish invention and its restrictions on instinctual wishes, both sexual and aggressive, were a continuation of Judaism.

Anti-semitism is an over-determined phenomenon which can be partly explained in terms of people disliking those who are successful, which Jews often are, and partly by 'the narcissism of minor differences' — the dislike and hatred of one group for those who are very similar but different from them. There are many unconscious factors too, like the jealousy of people towards the first-born and favourite child of the one and only God. There is also the fear of castration which is roused by the Jewish practice of circumcision among peoples who do not typically circumcise, or if they do still feel threatened by fuller castration. Freud, it must be remembered, uses the term castration to mean removal of the penis as well as the testicles, for this is what little boys fear most, and some little girls think this has been done to them when they compare themselves with boys.

The Jews have seen themselves as a special, chosen people. Freud analyses this as being due to their development of intellectuality (*Geistigkeit*) rather than sensuality; to the stress on ethics in the Judaism of the Prophets rather than sensual rituals, or physical prowess.

> The pre-eminence given to intellectual labours throughout some two thousand years in the life of the Jewish people has, of course, had its effect. It has helped to check the brutality and the tendency to violence which are apt to appear where the development of muscular strength is the popular ideal. Harmony in the cultivation of intellectual and physical activity, such as was achieved by the Greek people, was denied to the Jews. In this dichotomy their decision was at least in favour of the worthier alternative.[44]

Freud develops the idea of a move from the primal horde to matriarchy after the killing of the primal father by the band of brothers. The women were able to take some of the power and authority in the group because the sons were full of remorse for their parricide. In this period goddesses and their sons flourished in the development of religions. Christianity in its Orthodox and Catholic form retained this Mother–Son religious theme in the role preserved for Mary the Mother of Jesus. Protestantism marked a return to full patriarchy in the symbolic ritual practices of Christianity, with its stress on the Father, more than the Mother.

The Son takes on aspects of the primal father too — the Son who was killed by the Jews. Jesus was seen as the Messiah, even as a second Moses, and the Jews arranged to have him murdered as they had done the first Moses, the Egyptian Moses. Both were re-enactments of the killing of the primal father. They were acting out the return of the repressed rather than remembering it. This is something which neurotics in psychoanalytic therapy do when powerful material lies repressed and latent in the unconscious but which cannot be remembered in analytic sessions. The repressed returns but in actions rather than words and memories until the analysis is complete. The Jews have been compelled to repeat because they have remained in a latency phase; they will not acknowledge that they killed Moses, Jesus, or the primal father.

Judaism marked a turning away from matriarchy, from the mother and sensuality, to the father and intellectuality/spirituality. Freud explains that he means by this that maternity of a child is known through the senses and perceptions, but that paternity is 'a hypothesis, based on an inference and a premise'.[45] The Jews, unlike the Ancient Greeks, developed only this intellectual, ethical, spiritual side of themselves. They had renounced more direct instinctual gratifications than the Greeks or other ancient peoples. This instinctual renunciation produced in the Jews collectively the same sense of quiet superiority that the individual feels who has renounced an instinctual desire at the behest of the superego. The Jews felt superior because they renounced more aggressive and sexual instinctual wishes than others and in so doing thought they were obeying the will of God.

The ethical demands of the Prophets were prolongations of the will of the primal father: 'We confidently expect that an investigation of all other cases of sacred prohibition would lead to the same conclusion as in that of the horror of incest: that what is sacred was originally nothing other than the prolongation of the will of the primal father'.[46]

Freud claimed that he was able to use much of his understanding of the neuroses derived from psychoanalytic therapy and from analytic observations of children in developing his psychoanalytic theory of religion and society. In *Moses and Monotheism* he used his main psychoanalytic model of the aetiology of neurosis which assumed that there was an early traumatic experience in infancy which is handled by defences being set up to keep the memories and pains of the trauma repressed. The trauma lies latently in the unconscious. It may express itself again at puberty when sexual and aggressive instinctual pressures are too strong for the defences the child set up earlier. This second appearance comes in the form of symptoms which may persist into adulthood, or which may be resolved, or be repressed again. A religion may help the adolescent handle the return of the repressed material at this stage in their life-cycle development, and no doubt many conversions to various religious groups among adolescents and young adults can be understood in this way. The fundamental hypothesis which Freud used here to understand and explain the development of Judaism and Christianity is the notion of *the return of the repressed*.

In this way Freudian explanations of religious beliefs, symbols, rituals and organizational expressions of differences over theology can move beyond empirical descriptions of what has happened, and beyond tracing the economic and political class influences on these developments in the way a Marxist sociologist might do. Even if sociologists wish to reject Freudian explanations of religious and associated political phenomena, such as anti-semitism, they do need to take them seriously enough to examine them.

A second feature which Freud uses in his parallel between individual and group psychology as he calls it — that is his social theory — is the acquisition of culture, crucially language. The child is introduced to language especially between two and four years of age, and this affects the ways in which he or she handles their potentially truamatic experiences, and their researches into sexuality. When humans first moved from being higher animals to being recognizably human beings they produced cultures, and language. Freud shares the common assumption of most sociologists and anthropologists of the twentieth century that human cultures first developed rituals and symbols, such as totemism — the elementary form of religion. Language also developed in this early phase of human social evolution. The *archaic heritage* of mankind is contained, therefore, in religious symbols, beliefs, rituals and sacred books and in language. Psychoanalytic investigations into words or rituals, symbols and myths can reveal something of the archaic heritage which we have all acquired.

Each individual has access to the archaic heritage, not just through socialization into a particular language and religion, but also constitutionally. This may sound a horrifying idea, but Freud is concerned to say that the capacity to symbolize is innate in human beings.

> There is ... the universality of symbolism in language. The symbolic representation of one object by another — the same thing applies to actions — is familiar to all our children and comes to them, as it were, as a matter of course. We cannot show in regard to them how they have learnt it and must admit that in many cases learning it is impossible. It is a question of an original knowledge which adults afterwards forget. It is true that an adult makes use of the same symbols in his dreams, but he does not understand them unless an analyst interprets them.[47]

Freud goes on to say that religions can be seen as collective attempts to solve the problems which neuroses in the individual try to do — handling the return of the repressed, that is, the repressed instinctual desires of sexuality and destructive aggression. More than this, however, there is a part of the phylogenetic archaic heritage in each individual:

> When we study the reactions to early traumas, we are quite often surprised to find that they are not strictly limited to what the subject himself has really experienced but diverge from it in a way which fits in much better with the model of a phylogenetic event and, in general, can only be explained by such an influence. The behaviour of neurotic children towards their parents in the Oedipus and castration complex abounds in such reactions, which seems unjustified in the individual case and only becomes intelligible phylogenetically — by their connection with the experience of earlier generations.[48]

The archaic heritage concept bridges the gulf between individual and group psychology. It is to be understood as an instinct ('instinkt' was the word used in Freud's German, not his more usual 'Trieb') similar to the instinctive life of animals. Freud argued:

> The position in the human animal would not at bottom be different. His own archaic heritage corresponds to the instincts of animals even though it is different in its compass and contents. After this discussion I have no hesitation in declaring that men have always known (in this special way) that they once possessed a primal father and killed him.[49]

These ideas can appear to be far removed from contemporary scientific thought in either biology, sociology, anthropology or even later psychoanalysis. They have been discussed by some recent writers in both a critical and in a more favourable light as will be shown later. The analysis of the Jews and of Christianity, when linked with the work in *Totem and Taboo* and the other more sociological texts which have been presented in outline in this part of the book, provides the foundations for a substantial psychoanalysis of society and religion. Its full implications have still not been worked out, or worked through.

Freud's central concern can be seen to be with the development of human culture and society, and with the individual's acquisition of culture. Human cultures contain both language and religion as central components. Human societies consist of authority relationships, laws both written and unwritten, and related to both these factors there are class groups based on differential relations to work and the wealth of the society which the technology produces. Freud does not posit any relationship between cultures and structures of the kind Marx and Marxists have proposed. Rather Freud sees the instinctual balance between renunciation and gratification of instinctual wishes and desires as being fundamental in any society. As a part of this balance between the frustration and the satisfaction of sexual and destructive instinctual desires Freud sees religions, the arts and authority structures generally as having a central part to play. For those people who cannot find enough satisfaction for their instinctual wishes in the collective institutions of religion, work, art, and family there is the sick role — neurosis and associated symptoms.

Freud assumed that it is difficult for many people to attain the level of adult rational thinking and action which modern societies require. Modern societies, called by Freud 'civilization', require a great deal of instinctual renunciation, especially among the highly educated and among those who do much of the hard work. The amount of gratification of instinctual impulses may fall so low that civilization is rejected in favour of modern barbarism (as in Nazism).

As a conclusion to this chapter it is worth examining the last of the *New Introductory Lectures on Psychoanalysis* (Number 35).[50] Freud here discusses the question of whether psychoanalysis is itself a *Weltanschauung* (a world outlook; a philosophy of life.) He argues that it is not a separate *Weltanschauung* but is part of science. Science hardly deserves such a grand name as that — but psychoanalysis is content to be a part of the world outlook of science. It studies the workings and products of the human mind, both in its individual and collective forms. It must, therefore, study and try to explain collective productions of the mind such as religions, the arts, and philosophies. Science cannot rest content with the liberal and tolerant view that it is one way of looking at the world, alongside and equal to those of religion and philosophy. 'It is simply a fact that the truth cannot be tolerant, that it admits of no compromises or limitations, that research regards every sphere of human activity as belonging to it and that it must be relentlessly critical if any other power tries to take over any part of it.'[51] Freud's use of the term 'science' here is not very rigorous. He simply means to distinguish his work from irrational ideology.

Psychoanalysis must pursue its researches into religions, and this proves to be a more formidable task than research into the arts or philosophy. The arts and artists do not make claims to be dealing with reality; people know that the arts deal with emotions, wishes, and illusions. There is less conflict between science and the arts than between science and religions because the latter do claim to offer knowledge of reality as well as the sciences. The two compete with one another here. Philosophy competes less with science than does religion because it uses some of the same methods as the sciences — such as logical analysis of theoretical concepts — but it does nevertheless sometimes offer a systematic view of the whole universe on the basis of methods which are unscientific. Views of the universe arrived at by philosophical speculation and by intuition are liable to be refuted by the research of natural scientists.

Religions are based on the child's view of the world as having been created by a powerful parent figure (a mixture of father and mother) who is protective and comforting and who issues commands and rules which must be obeyed if the child is to avoid punishment and retain the love and protection of the parent — especially the father. There are three main functions of religions. They offer knowledge about the universe and how it came to be, thus satisfying the human desire for knowledge. Secondly, they offer comfort and consolation on an emotional level when life is cruel and hard on people. Thirdly, they provide ethical rules for conduct of interpersonal relationships. They can link these three together — the nature of the heavens and of life on earth, the emotional consolations, and the ethical moral rules — because their origin lies in the experiences of children in relation to their parents. Some religions stress the mother–child relationship, others the father–child relationship. Freud sees the latter as of great importance in the development of human civilization because religions orientated to the father as their central symbol have led to greater intellectuality, to a stress on ethical religion rather than ritualistic religion, and have therefore produced some growth towards rationality out of their illusory beliefs. There is here a similarity between Freud and Weber.

Psychoanalysis has furthered our understanding and the scientific explanation of the persistence and ubiquity of religion in human societies by tracing its roots back to childhood wishes and views of the world. Science offers much less emotional consolation than religion but it can offer some similar ethical principles, with the advantage that they are based on rational thought about man in society and not on illusory beliefs. The arts can and do provide some emotional consolation for people who have lost their religious faith, and their capacity to derive comfort and emotionally significant feelings from the rituals of the old religions. Modern human beings are struggling to live without the old religions; psychoanalysis can aid them to do so. It can offer a scientific theory of the workings of the human mind in the individual, and in the collective, based on its research into neuroses and on childrens' and primitives' ways of seeing the world. Therapy can help strengthen an adult's capacity to become more rational in their thought and action, and to be in more control of their feelings — especially the destructive ones towards the self.

Before religions developed there had been a phase of animism and magic, which has never disappeared from human societies. Indeed animism (beliefs in a world full of spirits, demons, and impersonal forces) and associated magical practices could be said to have grown again in modern societies. Both in Freud's lifetime and again in the last two or three decades, such animistic views of the world have become quite popular. There has been a renewed interest in astrology, in witchcraft and associated magical practices, in spiritualism and in faith healing.

This is not unrelated to intellectual nihilism — the view that science is an arbitrary way to knowledge, and that other ways are as good. Such a view denies the correspondence theory of truth, which Freud here assumes is basic to the sciences and reason, and often begins from the theory of relativity in science, but ends by rejecting science and making way for a return of religions and animism.

The recent work of P. Feyerabend in a book such as *Against Method* (1975) is of this kind. It takes no account of the importance of scientific reasoning for humanity; Feyerabend does consistently show the way back for animistic ways of thinking by including an astrological chart of the author on the book cover. It was a text illustrative of some intellectuals' discontents with modern civilization in the nineteen-seventies.

Freud outlines his position on Marx and Marxism in this last lecture too. He argues that although the economic factor is very important in societies, it cannot be seen as determining the development of culture. Cultures develop by means of instinctual renunciations and offering compensations for these repressed wishes, as he claims psychoanalysis has shown to some extent. This kind of psychological basis of culture cannot be as easily dismissed as it is in Marxism. Nor can human aggression be seen as being the product only of the arrangements of private property. Class relations can be altered and abolished, but aggression and violence towards others continue, as in the Soviet Union. The invention of gunpowder, and air power, have been as important in history as economic factors says Freud — admitting his point lies strictly outside the field of psychoanalysis, as indeed it does. Freud does say that the emphasis given to science and technology in Marx's work is important, but that it has been lost in the Soviet Union's attempts to control thought, especially the critical appraisal of Marxism, as strongly as the

Catholic Church tried to control thought about God and theology. This is a pity in Freud's view because the attempt to move beyond religion in the Soviet system was initially a step forward:

> At a time when the great nations announce that they expect salvation only from the maintenance of Christian piety, the revolution in Russia — in spite of all its disagreeable details — seems none the less like the message of a better future. Unluckily neither our scepticism nor the fanatical faith of the other side gives a hint as to how the experiment will turn out. The future will tell us; perhaps it will show that the experiment was undertaken prematurely, that a sweeping alteration of the social order has little prospect of success until new discoveries have increased our control over the forces of Nature and so made easier the satisfaction of our needs. Only then perhaps may it become possible for a new social order not only to put an end to the material need of the masses but also to give a hearing to the cultural demands of the individual. Even then, to be sure, we shall still have to struggle for an incalculable time with the difficulties which the untameable character of human nature presents to every kind of social community.[52]

NOTES AND REFERENCES

[1] S. Freud, *Beyond the Pleasure Principle* (1920), Standard Edition, Volume 18, Hogarth Press, London (1961).
[2] Ibid., section 3.
[3] Ibid., section 2.
[4] Ibid., section 5.
[5] Ibid., section 5, p. 78.
[6] S. Freud, *The Ego and the Id* (1923), Standard Edition, Volume 19, Hogarth Press, London (1962).
[7] Ibid., Chapter 2, p. 15.
[8] Ibid., Chapter 5, p. 43.
[9] Discussed in Chapter 2, section 'Morality'.
[10] S. Freud, *Leonardo da Vinci and a Memory of his Childhood* (1910), Standard Edition, Volume 11, Hogarth Press, London.
[11] S. Freud, *Totem and Taboo* (1912-13), Standard Edition, Volume 13, Hogarth Press, London (1950). References to Routledge & Kegan Paul, London (1960) edition.

[12] For a discussion of Lévi-Strauss and Freud see C. Badcock, *Lévi-Strauss; Structuralism and Sociological Theory,* Chapter 5, Hutchinson (1975).
[13] S. Freud, p. 4, *Totem and Taboo,* (see reference in note 11 above).
[14] Ibid., p. 18.
[15] Ibid., p. 31.
[16] Ibid., p. 42.
[17] Ibid., p. 88.
[18] Ibid., p. 82.
[19] Ibid., p. 132.
[20] Ibid., p. 141.
[21] Ibid., p. 142.
[22] Ibid., p. 144.
[23] Ibid., p. 145.
[24] S. Freud, *Group Psychology and the Analysis of the Ego* (1921), Standard Edition, Volume 18, Hogarth Press, London (1959).
[25] Ibid., pp. 10–11.
[26] See F. Parkin, *Max Weber,* Key Sociologists Series, Ellis Horwood/Tavistock, London and Methuen, New York (1982), pp. 84–7.
[27] S. Freud, *Group Psychology* (see note 24 above), p. 48.
[28] Ibid., Chapter 9.
[29] Ibid., pp. 52–3.
[30] S. Freud, *Negation* (1925), Standard Edition, Volume 19, Hogarth Press, London (1962).
[31] S. Freud, *The Future of an Illusion* (1927), Standard Edition, Volume 21, Hogarth Press, London (1962).
[32] Ibid., p. 3.
[33] Ibid., p. 26.
[34] Ibid., p. 45.
[35] Ibid., p. 49.
[36] Ibid., p. 52.
[37] S. Freud, *Civilization and its Discontents* (1930), Standard Edition, Volume 21, Hogarth Press, London (1963).
[38] Ibid., p. 49.
[39] Ibid., p. 50.
[40] Ibid., p. 52.
[41] Ibid., p. 71.
[42] Ibid., p. 80.
[43] S. Freud, *Moses and Monotheism* (1939), Standard Edition, Volume 23, Hogarth Press, London (1964, corrected 1974).
[44] Ibid., p. 115.

[45] Ibid., p. 114.
[46] Ibid., p. 121.
[47] Ibid., p. 98.
[48] Ibid., p. 99.
[49] Ibid., p. 100-1.
[50] S. Freud, *New Introductory Lectures On Psychoanalysis* (1933, 1932), Standard Edition, Volume 22, Hogarth Press, London (1964); New York (1966); The Pelican Freud Library, Volume 2, Penguin, Harmondsworth (1973). References are to this Pelican edition, Lecture Number 35.
[51] Ibid., p. 195.
[52] Ibid., pp. 218-19.

4

Methods and Methodology

The use of analysis for the treatment of neurosis is only one of its applications; the future will perhaps show that it is not the most important one. S. Freud [1]

Many of the disagreements about psychoanalysis and its relevance to sociology reflect wider issues about the methodology which is considered to be most appropriate to the study of human actions. It is important to consider some of the main methodological points which affect the ways in which sociologists and social theorists have approached psychoanalysis. But first the criticism that psychoanalysis is unscientific needs mentioning.

PSYCHOANALYSIS AS 'SCIENCE'

The philosopher Karl Popper claims that a science advances by trying to *falsify* hypotheses, not by seeking to *confirm* them empirically. The problem with psychoanalytic propositions from this perspective is that like those of Marxism they are *unfalsifiable* — there is nothing which can count against them. Psychoanalysts, it is held, can always say that someone who rejects a particular psychoanalytic proposition is doing so for unconscious motives. Such propositions are unfalsifiable. No argument can ever count against them, no evidence can refute such propositions, on this view. The analysts can always win an argument by using this stratagem. Anyone arguing against psychoanalytic ideas is said to be defending against unconscious feelings by analysts, so the very arguments used to refute psychoanalysis by its opponents actually confirm it in the eyes of analysts. This basic assumption of psychoanalysis has to be accepted as an article of faith and then all human actions and arguments are interpreted within it. Psychoanalysis is, therefore, a closed belief system, not open-ended to Popper and Popperians.[2]

Such an argument as that of Popper does not do justice to the ways in which psychoanalysis actually operates in theory and practice. Far from being a closed belief system psychoanalysis is open enough to accept a variety of positions within it about many fundamental issues, such as the universality of Oedipus which is accepted by some and rejected by others.

The concept of the unconscious, however, is not simply a proposition which could be falsified as the Popperian position assumes. It is a basic founding concept of an area of research. It is a fundamental concept of psychoanalysis in the sense that it *founds* the subject. Psychoanalysis is a theory and a method for the investigation of the unconscious and its ways of working.

The unconscious is not a thing but an area which is conceptually produced. It has to be investigated using particular methods. To say the area of the unconscious is conceptually produced is not to rule out psychoanalysis as unscientific because other sciences do the same thing. The area of investigation of sub-atomic physics, for example, is conceptually produced too.

A conceptually produced area of investigation relates in quite complex ways to specific empirically observable phenomena. The area for investigation must relate to empirical observations of some kind otherwise the subject becomes like theology. Theology does have a conceptual area to investigate, the relations between God and mankind, but it has a highly ambiguous relationship to empirical observations.

The concept of the unconscious does relate to observable phenomena of a particular kind. The phenomena are not just given to the senses of the observer in psychoanalysis any more than occurs in other sciences. They are in part created by the conceptual framework being used to make some things more significant than others for the observer. In the case of the unconscious the major way into gaining some knowledge about its workings was through the interpretation of the *meaning* of dreams. Psychoanalysis is not trying to contribute to the whole of a scientific theory of dreams. This is a perfectly possible area of research, but it is not the same as psychoanalytic investigation into the meaning of a dream. To this extent psychoanalysis is a hermeneutic discipline concerned with the interpretation of meanings.[3]

Psychoanalysis is also concerned to interpret the meaning of symptoms which had formerly been seen either as accidents, or peculiar traits of a person, or as signs that someone was possessed by a devil, a spell, or even a god. Freud had begun his career as a natural scientist interested in the human nervous system. It took him some years to realize that human beings could and did attach meanings to their actions, not in the same sense as Weber had meant in his sociology, but meanings which the person themselves did not find easy to put into words. People find that they do do some things, such as sleep walking, or repeatedly chasing after girls or boys for love affairs, or wanting to give up cigarettes or alcohol but being unable to do so, which are puzzling to them. They may not be able to give a reason for their actions, and may find them unclear in meaning but think nevertheless that they do have a meaning. These sorts of phenomena were seen as unimportant to the human sciences before Freud. They are still seen as unimportant by those who have not integrated Freud into their understanding of human beings.

Among those who are willing to examine Freudian theory from within the context of social theory and sociology there is unfortunately no unanimity about what counts as a contribution to the social sciences. There are some who hold for example that sociology and social theory do *necessarily* involve political standpoints. It is not just a lapse when some sociologist is seen as having a political standpoint — it is inherent in any description or analysis of the social world whatsoever. Given this it is better to be explicit about one's political standpoint, as Marxists are for instance, than to purport to be doing value-neutral social science. The conservative stance behind such an attempt can always be pointed out by those committed to change, as has been the case in the way many radical sociologists perceived the sociology of Talcott Parsons.

Critical theorists of the Frankfurt School have maintained that in the study of the social, political values are inherently involved. They have aimed therefore, not to develop a value-neutral social science in the way Weber and Durkheim are though to have aimed to do, but to produce a theory which is rational. In such a theory the value of rationality is the basis of the political and ethical values, and leads to a critique of those institutions, political, religious, educational, cultural and economic, which continue to maintain irrational patterns of action. The approach to Freud, like the approach to Marx, which is taken by critical theorists, lays stress on the ways in which both theories examine the forces which maintain irrationally in social interaction. Both Marx and Freud are seen by critical theorists as committed to the value of rationality. This is not an ahistorical notion of philosophical reason, but a concept of reason which changes from one type of society to another, from one historical period to another. However, critical theorists are anxious to avoid complete relativism, and hence insist that there are more universal rational values than relativism allows. Marx and Freud both reocgnized this.

On the other hand are structuralist conceptions of social science which reflect certain positions derived from linguistics. These ideas of doing science emphasize synchronic rather diachronic dimensions, that means that the ahistorical structure of language, myth, the unconscious (as in Lacan) is seen as being capable of being studied objectively, that is scientifically. The more historicist approach to social science typical of critical theory is criticized by structuralists for being hopelessly unscientific and unobjective. Such a viewpoint leads to a very different version of Freud from that of either Parsons or of the critical theorists. The unconscious is emphasized by the structuralist reading of Freud, which is not the case in the Parsonian use of psychoanalysis. However, unlike the critical theorists, who also emphasize the unconscious, structuralists do not see Freud as a contributor to a social theory based on rationality. The notion of rationality is too teleological and linked with a false view of human subjectivity for structuralists. Yet for critical theorists structuralism would appear to be another false and unwise attempt to develop the impossible – an ahistorical, objective, science of society and culture.

As has been indicated in the earlier chapters of this book Freud used a conception of rationality both in the way in which he constructed and changed his theory, and in his understanding of the working of the ego, the part of the mind concerned with rational thinking and reality-testing. Without some such concept it is difficult to escape complete determinism in psychoanalysis for there is no way of breaking the impasse of unconscious determinants on actions and on thinking. Equally, without some concept of rationality the aim of psychoanalytic therapy is unclear. Unless there is the possibility of increasing the rationality of someone's thought and action about themselves and the world around them, it is difficult to see what therapy can aim at other then uncovering the unconscious determinants on the person. Critical theorists have been correct to stress this in their appropriation of

Freudian theory and practice. This does not rule out accepting the degree to which non-rationality and irrationality exist and operate in societies and in human social actions, because it was this that they were trying to understand in the first place by turning to Freud's theory of unconscious motivations for action.

SOCIOLOGY AND PSYCHOANALYSIS IN THE UNITED STATES

In the United States sociologists' views of Freud have been influenced to a considerable extent by the work of Talcott Parsons, who tried to integrate Freudian concepts of socialization with his sociology. He was particularly struck by similarities between Freud's work and that of Durkheim in that both of them stressed processes concerned with the internationalization of symbols.

> In Durkheim's work there are only suggestions relative to the psychological mechanisms of internationalization and the place of internalized moral values in the structure of personality itself. But this does not detract from the massive phenomenon of the convergence of the fundamental insights of Freud and Durkheim, insights not only as to the fundamental importance of moral values in human behaviour, but of the internalization of these values. This convergence, from two quite distinct and independent starting points, deserves to be ranked as one of the truly fundamantal landmarks of the development of modern social science.[4]

In one of his very last papers Parsons wrote about the similarities between the sociology of Weber and Freud.[5] He laid stress here on the analysis they both made of rationality and its relation to the non-rational. In both Freud's work on the ego and its relation with external reality, and in Weber's on instrumental rationality, there is a concern with rational thought and action. Both also emphasize the instability of rational action, and Parsons suggests parallels between the id impulses in Freud and Weber's notion of charisma for they both are concepts which introduce an element of the non-rational into human action. Parsons did not develop any links between Weber's sociology of religion, and of charismatic figures in religions, and Freud's work on religion and father figures such as Moses and Jesus. This is by no means unusual in the way Parsons approached Freud.

Throughout his writings on Freud, Parsons emphasizes the theory of personality in Freud, that is the id, ego, superego model. He tends to isolate this both from the instinct theory, prefering the notion of id-impulse to that of instinctual desire, and from the theory of social evolution and of religion in Freud. Parsons approached Freud through American and British psychoanalysts and this entailed both the lack of emphasis on sexuality and the death instincts and the omission of the theory of society and culture Freud had developed. Analysts were not unnaturally primarily concerned with the theory of personality and with therapy, but sociologists and anthropologists could be expected to at least mention the other more social theory in Freud's work, even if rejecting it in the last analysis. This Parsons failed to do and this fact has had serious consequences for some later sociologists who have tried to use psychoanalytic ideas and sociology in their work.

The work of F. Weinstein and G. Platt, as in *Psychoanalytic Sociology* (1973), develops the Parsonian legacy, but in a direction which moves away from the instinct theory and the social theory in Freud. They, and Parsons himself, end up in a position which ignores the founding concept of psychoanalysis: the unconscious. Psychoanalytic sociology of this kind can yield a social psychology which operates mainly on the pre-conscious and conscious levels of personality, culture and social system.

In Parsons the emphasis Freud had given to *conflict* is lessened to the point of extinction. Conflicts between instinctual wishes of both a destructive aggressive and sexually perverse kind and the internalized values of the society, or the external social control agents, which were central for Freud, are eroded. This happens because Parsons, and those influenced by him, assume that culture codes emotions and feelings to such an extent that there is no instinctual source of emotions remaining in the theory. There is no instinctual id-impulse as such, which is independent of learned and internalized cultural symbols. All the aspects of the personality — id, ego and superego — are produced by socialization for Parsons. This theory is certainly not the same as Freud's.

The influence of Parsons continues to affect the way a recent author analyses the sociology of gender and tries to use psychoanalysis in doing so. Nancy Chodorow in an important book *The Reproduction of Mothering* (1978)[6] uses the British and American object-relations school of psychoanalysis and tries to integrate this with a sociology of gender, especially in understanding the reproduction of mothering among women. Her aim is to work out how it would be possible for men to be seen by themselves, and others, as capable of mothering as well as women. This topic is one which does need both sociological and psychoanalytic theory applied to it, and Nancy Chodorow is wise to try to do this. Others have criticized her for bringing in psychoanalysis at all, but in an area such as this some conceptualization of the roots of gender identity seems necessary. Most men will not conceive of them-selves as people who can mother babies and children on fully equal terms with women. There are many non-rational issues involved here about masculinity, feminity, mothering, the breast, and the relations between men and women. Chodorow is quite right to turn to psycho-analysis for a vocabulary to help fill out the more sociological analysis she gives. It is unfortunate, therefore, that she has under-played the role of the *unconscious* in this area of the reproduction of mothering. It is not entirely absent, but it is almost sociologized away, as Parsons had done previously. The object-relations approach within psycho-analysis stresses social relations between parents and children, and later between adults and the child, but it does retain a concern with un-conscious processes involved in these relationships, as did Freud. Parsons and those influenced by him, however indirectly, tend to miss this emphasis on the unconscious, but without it there is little point in sociologists turning to psychoanalysis.

CLINICAL METHOD AND PSYCHOANALYTIC THEORY

One major problem with Freud's methods from the point of view of some sociologists is psychoanalysts' over-reliance on the clinical method. To psychoanalysts themselves the clinical method is the only one which can be used legitimately in developing and changing psychoanalytic theory. This view has been adopted by some writers with a more sociological approach such as Erich Fromm and, more recently, by Nancy Chodorow. Those sociologists influenced by either an historical approach to sociology, or a comparative approach, or a statistical survey approach, may well find problems with the clinical method.

Very often major changes are made to psychoanalytic theory on the basis of a single case history. This is true of Freud's own work, and of later psychoanalysts. Such a method seems to ignore questions about how typical a particular case is of its kind, and with whether the same thing would be found among different classes, cultures, or histori-cal periods. Sociologists have often asserted that psychoanalysis is based on twentieth-century middle class, Western, Judaeo-Christian people with psychological problems, not even 'normal' people from this group. If this is so, it is claimed, it invalidates any claims psychoanalysis makes to be a universal theory about the workings of the mind.

These criticisms depend on a particular view of what it is that psychoanalytic theory is trying to achieve. There is no unanimity among psychoanalysts about this, however, let alone among sociologists and social theorists. For some psychoanalysts, and those sociologists such as Talcott Parsons who accept the same version, the aim of psycho-analysis is to develop a theory of human personality. Personality is seen as an attribute of individuals — a set of typical capacities and ways of responding to problems and to other people which each person can be seen to possess or to use. This can be considered to be either a part of what Freud was trying to do, or, mistakenly, the whole of it.

Talcott Parsons, and later writers influenced by him such as Wein-stein and Platt and Chodorow, treat Freud's personality theory as a contribution to social science, but have usually treated the social theory and the theory of religion as poor science, and the weakest part of psychoanalysis. This assessment is sometimes shared by those who might be described as taking a broadly structuralist position, such as Juliet Mitchell in *Psychoanalysis and Feminism* (1974), although she does treat psychoanalysis as a theory about personality and gender in *patriarchal* societies.

Clearly Freud was not just concerned with developing a set of personality types which may be found in modern societies, some of which are still found, and some of which have disappeared with the passing of the years. There is a theory of group psychology, of civiliza-tion, morality, art, and religion in Freud's writings, as well as a theory of the individual workings of the mind.

There are some psychoanalysts who have tried to develop the more anthropological and social aspects of psychoanalysis such as Eric Fromm, Wilhelm Reich and Geza Roheim. There are some social theorists, or sociologists, who have done the same. Herbert Marcuse is perhaps the best known, but not the only one to do so.

Jaques Lacan, and some of his pupils and followers, would also claim that Freud had developed a theory about culture, especially language, which can now be better understood after certain advances in linguistics made since Freud. Some who take this structuralist position systematically remove the notion of the individual self, or personality, from their understanding of psychoanalysis. They claim that psychoanalysis is a theory about the unconscious — and the unconscious as a concept removes the notion of there being a person as an active conscious agent. Instead the emphasis is placed upon the unconscious as a structure which displaces subjectivity, personality, the self, the individual, and all such notions. The notions of the per-sonality, or the self, or the true self, which are used by some versions of humanistic psychology and allied therapies, are rejected by Lacanians as betraying the gains made by Freud in his concept of the unconscious. These gains were over notions of the soul — a concept which belongs to religious discourse and to philosophies based on the spirit as being more real than matter (usually called 'idealist' philosophies). It is not insignificant that the new humanistic psychologies and associated therapies are typically uncritical towards religions of all kinds. The concepts of the personality, or the self, even in social science, are concepts which are secular derivatives from the religious notion of the soul, or spirit. Freud's advance consisted in moving beyond this kind of conceptualization of human beings, and his concept of the unconscious, unlike that of Carl Jung, was based on materialistic science and not on religion's notion of souls and spirits. These points which have been made by structuralists such as Lacan do help to clarify matters about the advance made by Freud in this context.

To return to the criticisms of psychoanalytic clinical method. Judgements about this methodological question are not possible outside the wider issues which have just been discussed about the aims of psychoanalysis as a science. Freud was trying to develop a science of the unconscious. This unconscious operates in individuals and in the collective groups in which human beings live. There is no need to introduce a term such as the 'collective unconscious' as Jung proposed, because there is just one unconscious which is indistinguishable in individuals and in groups in the ways in which it works. There are collective unconscious elements in individuals, especially in the super-ego. And there are individual unconscious processes at work in group leaders — who are indispensable in the Freudian concept of human groups based as it is on the idea of the primal horde, and the primal father.

Given that psychoanalysis is attempting to develop a new area of research, that of the unconscious in individuals and in groups, the judgement about the role of clinical method becomes easier to make. The method of psychoanalytic therapy is the major research instrument for investigating the unconscious.

This therapeutic group of two is unlike any other group in that the therapist does not interact in a usual fashion, but from the point of view of the therapee it is like another group, namely his or her family of origin. Therapy is a method of researching the unconscious, using the transference in the group of two. (Group therapy can also reveal important material about the unconscious workings of larger groups. The Tavistock Institute in London has used group methods in researching the unconscious in work groups.) Clinical research uses more than one single case, although one case may be used to illustrate a point found in a number of case histories.

Psychoanalysis had to begin somewhere, sometime, with a specific set of people. Undoubtedly the time, place, and social, cultural, historical setting of its first researches into the unconscious have affected psycho-analytic theory. It should be remembered, however, that Freud did use anthropological material in his theorization of the social and cultural development of human beings. Although he did not visit pre-literate peoples, others trained in psychoanalysis, have done so since.

Many therapists and psychoanalysts now aim only to achieve thera-peutic results — by no means an unworthy aim — but many of them have given up trying to develop the general theory of the unconscious. They aim to give some relief to distressed people, and anything that can do this is seen as useful in therapy no matter from which school of theory the therapy derives. This pragmatic approach was not Freud's approach. He was interested in therapeutic success like any other medically trained doctor or modern therapist. But he was also trying to develop in a reasonably systematic way *the theory* for the new science of the unconscious. The clinical method was the main one available. It enabled him to gain some basic knowledge about the unconscious in people who had symptoms and states of mind which revealed its workings more clearly than in so-called normal people. Freud thought that it was only a matter of degree involved here, that 'normal' people used similar unconscious mechanisms to those used by neurotics and psychotics. The unconscious workings were easier to observe in those who were being over-powered by them in their lives. His clinical method had the advantage over some academic methods of interviewing in that it could sometimes relieve unnecessary human suffering. It also has some similarities to the life-history interview method, which is now being used again by some sociologists interested in gender and sexuality for instance.

Therapy was not Freud's only method. He had started the deve-lopment of psychoanalysis in his studies of hysteria, but he also studied dreams — his own, as well as those of friends and therapees. He studied the workings of the unconscious in ordinary life — in slips of the tongue and pen, in forgetting names, and in jokes. Freud made use of observa-tions of children and talked to them. His studies of children were sometimes done as case histories, sometimes used to illustrate a point he wanted to make. As has just been mentioned he used the work of anthropologists, and he also made use of the work of historians and archaeologists on ancient civilizations. Added to this he would often quote from literature — from Sophocles, Shakespeare, and Goethe, for example.

Freud also used the work of fellow psychoanalysts to develop his theory; references to Ferenczi, Rank, Jones, and Klein can be found in his major texts on social theory, for instance. The events of politics and history of his own lifetime were also not just an influence on him but also suggested problems for psychoanalytic theory — especially human destructive aggression and violence. Last, but not least, Freud used religious myths, symbols and rituals as source material for developing his psychoanalytic theory of the unconscious.

So although the clinical method was a fundamental method for Freud, it was not the only one used to generate problems, concepts and theories. He used many sources of empirical material to try to confirm his theories, and even to try to refute them (at least as much as some natural scientists do when developing a new theory).

Freud also employed more purely theoretical methods in developing psychoanalysis. He would be worried about particular theoretical propositions and change them to make the theory more internally consistent. This was what he did when he found he needed to introduce the notion of the death instincts — for by using a concept of this kind he was able to make psychoanalysis more internally consistent and more powerful as an explanatory theory of otherwise puzzling and inexplicable phenomena.

Theory building is usually seen today as a key achievement and Freud is one of the major theory builders in social science. As such the weaknesses of his methods by contemporary standards of scholarship are more easily forgiven by some who think he did achieve a great amount in delineating a new area of research, providing a new method of investigating it, and building up the beginnings of a theory of the unconscious.

Theoretical debates are often better settled by conceptual analysis than by an appeal to spurious facts, and by using the notions of rationality, consistency, and freedom from internal contradiction, in judging between various theories. This is possible as long as there are some generally agreed criteria about what counts as rationality, absence of contradiction, consistency and explanatory power. In spite of the babble of confusing voices which have been heard in recent decades, and the flirtation with dialectical reasoning in Sartrean existential Marxism and psychoanalysis there is some agreement about these criteria of reasoning in any given historical era. Freud also saw this as a method alongside his clinical method and other more empiricist methods he used at times. As was shown in the outline and discussion of *The Future of an Illusion* Freud was committed to reason, science, to the Greek god Logos.

Psychoanalytic therapy has been seen not as a method of gaining knowledge for a wider scientific community but as a situation of enlightenment for the analysand. The analysand comes to learn how their own distorted understandings of themselves, and their distorted communications with other people, have arisen. Through this process of self-reflection change occurs. The change is the mark of the work of self-reflection having been done satisfactorily; it does not occur as a result of acquiring new intellectual knowledge about theory.

This model of psychoanalytic therapy is treated by Jurgen Habermas as the model of a critical theory.[7] The kind of systematic self-reflection that occurs in psychoanalytic therapy is *the* example of enlightenment — a form of knowledge which is distinct from scientific knowledge because it transforms the knower.

There are difficulties with Habermas's version of psychoanalysis, however, and with his notion of self-reflection in therapy as a paradigm for critical theory. Habermas underestimates the importance of instinctual desires in his version of Freudian psychoanalysis. Psychoanalysis is not just about the meanings of words and communications of a distorted kind, such as those of physical symptoms. It also contains a social theory, which Habermas does discuss, but which he does not fully connect with the instinct theory and with repression of instinctual desires. It is also difficult to see quite how therapy can be a paradigm of a critical *social* theory. There is no obvious equivalent of the psychotherapeutic encounter for social institutions. For therapy to be *the* science of self-reflection some way of doing the therapy of social institutions is needed, and in spite of some attempts at family therapy, there are no equivalents so far for either economic, legal, political or religious institutions. Some social changes made in educational institutions in the nineteen-sixties were seen by some as approaching the equivalent of psychotherapy for an institution such as a university or college, but the general assembly is hardly the same thing as a therapeutic encounter. There is confusion in the minds of some between the role of a therapist in a transference situation and that of a leader instructing someone how to change for the better. Therapeutic encounters are non-directive and non-judgemental. Speeches in meetings are neither non-directive nor non-judgemental.

Habermas has attempted to take his version of critical theory a stage further in his work on the ideal speech situation.[8] This is a situation derived from the social theories of Marx and Freud in which, for example, there is a relationship of equal power and wealth between those communicating, and in which people are aware of the unconscious forces which operate in groups. The notion of the ideal speech situation is not intended to be an empirical description of any social situation, but a model to aid analysis of social and cultural changes. Changes which are, as it were, inspired by the ideal speech situation are progressive and civilizing changes. Others may be designed to move away from allowing institutions such as universities, political parties, publishers of books and newspapers, or groups in churches to approach the ideal speech situation. Elites in some societies continue to try to prevent freedom of speech and writing because they seek to preserve a particular religious or political dogma and ideology. So Habermas's theory is not just an abstraction — it does produce concrete results in terms of political and social philosophy. These results led some to say Habermas had become a 'liberal' as though this were a term of abuse. His work does preserve the advances of modern liberalism and he is right to do this. He is less adequate in using psychoanalysis to help understanding of the forces of the irrational which operate in societies. These had been conceptualized to begin with in Freud's social theory of the primal horde, the primal father, and the archaic heritage.

The earlier generation of Frankfurt School critical theorists, such as Adorno and Marcuse, had tried to develop Freudian theory in this way. Even in the work of Reich and Fromm attempts were being made to develop Freud's ideas, but without the central notion of the death instincts their work is not using the full Freudian theory of society and groups. Marcuse and Adorno insisted that the more extreme propositions in Freud's theoretical works were the most valuable for critical theory, and this included for them the theory of polymorphously perverse infantile sexuality and the destructive death instinct theory. They argued that any critical theory must preserve the criticism of bourgeois society and culture made by Freud, and the emergent critique of socialism and communism in Freud.

The Freudian critique of bourgeois sexual morality, and bourgeois religion, must be maintained and developed. The Freudian analysis of authority and authoritarianism in both bourgeois and communist societies should likewise be developed.

The Freudian idea that socialism and communism were secular versions of Judaeo-Christian religions; that they could set up a cultural superego as repressive as that of some forms of these religions; that such regimes try to arrange for a school-playground notion of fairness and equality to be the basis of political economy, also need developing. Marcuse did this in his *Soviet Marxism* (1958) to an extent, and more recently Badcock (1980) has made the Freudian analysis of socialism and communism much more explicit, even though he writes from outside the paradigm of critical theory.

Yet if traditional religion is weak, and likely to weaken progressively, the prognosis with regard to other forms of social psychopathology is not so encouraging. In fact, far from disappearing, the underlying mass-psychopathology of Christianity is still strongly present, masquerading under the name of socialism.

It is a matter of common knowledge that Saint Simon, the inventor of socialism, originally called it 'New Christianity', and regarded it essentially as the Sermon on the Mount, shorn of all supernatural elements. As such, modern socialism enshrines the values of altruism found in the New Testament, but translated into a wholly materialist and worldly equivalent of traditional Christian moral masochism.[9]

The practice of psychoanalysis as a therapeutic technique has moved a long way since Freud's own work — but not always for the better. There has been an enormous growth in psychotherapy and counselling services in Western societies since Freud's death in 1939. It is true that not all of this work seeks its inspiration directly in Freud. But in such an area as this opposing someone's ideas and practices, as some think of themselves doing in relation to Freud, often belies an influence still operating in the act of opposition. Sociologists have been able to throw considerable light on the kinds of social economic and cultural influences which have led therapists, analysts, counsellors and social workers to try to change Freud's theory and practice in the direction of social conformity. Freud's own work is much more critical than later therapeutic techniques have become. For example, in the area of religious institutions, Freud was interested in tracing the damaging effects religion could have on some people, as well as the slight therapeutic gains of religious rituals. However, it is the latter, the supposed therapeutic gains which have been developed by many since, starting with Carl Jung. Freud's critical approach to religion, especially to the sexual morality of orthodox Judaism and ascetic Christianity, has been largely abandoned in practical terms as more and more clergy and church workers have become trained as counsellors.

Sociologists and anthropologists have often seen Freud's theory of religion as being too value-laden in the direction of the criticism of religion and of its sexual morality. The work of the American sociologist Peter Berger is a case in point. He is sometimes very perceptive about the way the society of the United States has distorted psychotherapy for its own purposes of success and achievement, but he is critical of Freud's overall theory, especially of religion. However, Berger is not himself value free, or free from theological commitments.
[10]

A recent book by C. Badcock uses Freudian theory and concepts to develop a critical approach to religion in human societies. Badcock relies on data from physical anthropology, animal ethology and sociobiology and assumes that data can be unproblematically transferred from one discipline to another, which is a big assumption to make.

Badcock has argued in *The Psychoanalysis of Culture* (1980) that Freud's work on society and culture should be seen as based on a case history — the case of mankind as a species. Culture is seen as centrally developed out of religious beliefs, symbols and rituals which are in turn analysed as being collective attempts to handle neuroses. The neuroses of the species arose out of the period when *homo sapiens* experienced the primal trauma — the killing of the primal fathers in the primal horde. This trauma lies at the root of human cultures, and can still be seen in religions, especially in Christianity.

Badcock argues that this theory of Freud's can be supported by new work in sociobiology and animal ethology. In particular he refers to the work of C. Jolly (1970) on gelada baboons who live in an environment similar to that of early man, namely savannah grassland. The gelada baboon's social organization 'consists of a large adult male, a group of females ... variable numbers of juvenile animals, infants and babies'. There are also all-male groups which move independently of the other type of group in which none of the adult males has a harem of females.[11]

There are reasons for seeing the gelada baboon as an immediate ancestor of *homo sapiens,* such as the fact that both species can pick up cereal seeds with a finger and thumb, and the dentition of both is similar. It is not, therefore, too far-fetched to think that the social organization of *homo sapiens* was of the primal horde, band of brothers type, as suggested by Darwin and Atkinson and used by Freud. Young male gelada baboons will fight older males for possession of some of his females. There is no evidence that the younger male gelada cooperate to do this and so become strong enough to kill the old males. This is the first step in the development of specifically human society in Freud's theory of the band of brothers.

Badcock also discusses the crucial claim Freud makes that the archaic heritage is inherited; that is that each new generation of human beings has an inherited memory of killing the primal father. He argues that modern sociobiology can help here:

Sociobiology has shown us just how problematic and unobvious the evolution of human social behaviour is. In the elaboration of his social structures, the degree of the development of his altruism, and the extent of the specialization of his corporate behaviour, man is only comparable with the social insects. Yet, phylogenetically, man is descended from notably unaltruistic species, and is related to living ones whose level of social development falls far below that found in the insect world ... The great strength of the theory propounded by Freud in *Totem and Taboo,* and elaborated in these pages, is that it explains the origin of altruism and social cooperation in man by means of typically human (i.e. psychological) process which, although very different from the genetically determined and automatic social responses of the lower animals, are nevertheless in their net effect closely comparable. The soldier ant, which kills itself in defending its nest, and the human soldier who dies on the battlefield for his country are manifesting exactly comparable behaviours. Yet each is motivated quite differently, and it is to the explanation of the peculiarly human in social behaviour that psychoanalysis can most successfully apply itself.[12]

Sociologists usually criticize arguments like those of Badcock for being reductionist, that is reducing society to another level of analysis whether this be psychological states in individuals, or biological factors. In Badcock's defence it should be pointed out that in anthropology recourse is made to biological and psychological factors, such as the innate way the human brain thinks in binary terms, that is thinking in terms of zero/one, or yes/no, in the work of Lévi-Strauss for example.

There is here a difference between sociologists and anthropologists in that the former are keener to avoid reductionism than the latter, although both disciplines have been influenced by Durkheim from whom many sociologists would derive their arguments against biological and psychological reductionism. The other influence on sociologists in this matter has been Marx, who has had less influence on anthropologists. Even so the French anthropologist Lévi-Strauss claims to be a Marxist, or a neo-Marxist.

The explanation for sociologists' concern to be pure and distinct may lie in the different academic histories of the two disciplines, certainly in Britain, where anthropology has long been accepted as an academic discipline in its own right at Oxford and Cambridge universities. Sociology has been the newcomer, only being properly established in the decades since 1950 in Britain, and then not really accepted in Oxford and Cambridge. This has made sociologists particularly anxious to stress the unique contribution their discipline can make to the study of man, and to de-emphasize its similarities to any other discipline. Anthropology, having been longer established as a pursuit of gentlemen and gentleladies, has been less self-conscious of a need to stress its uniqueness as a discipline, until recently at least.

In the United States the situation has been much more mixed, with a strong tradition of psychoanalytic anthropology being developed there. This has aided the development of a more integrative approach between sociology, anthropology, and psychoanalysis which reached a point of great importance in the work of Talcott Parsons. This has continued to be developed in the United States. Quite distinct from this has been the continuation of the work of critical theory and its use of Freudian theory by some American social scientists. Unlike the Parsonian tradition, the critical theoretical one is not divorced from Marx and Marxism but rather is a development of it. A recent writer influenced by critical theory, Russell Jacoby, has analysed the way in which Freudian theory has been forgotten in the United States especially. In *Social Amnesia* (1975) he wrote:

> The history of philosophy is the history of forgetting: so T. W. Adorno has remarked. Problems and ideas once examined fall out of sight and out of mind only to resurface later as novel and new. If anything the process seems to be intensifying; society remembers less and less faster and faster. The sign of the times is thought that has succumbed to fashion; it scorns the past as antiquated while touting the present as the best. Psychology is hardly exempt. What was known to Freud, half-remembered by the neo-Freudians, is unknown to their successors. The forgetfulness itself is driven by an unshakeable belief in progress: what comes later is necessarily better than what came before. Today, without romanticizing the past, one could almost state the reverse: what is new is worse than what is old.[13]

CONCLUSION: SOME FINAL REFLECTIONS

Freud's psychoanalytic theory and method contains important concepts and ideas about socialization into gender roles and about sexuality. There is a critical theory of religion and social groups linked with a more general theory about the development of human societies and their struggle to attain and retain civilization.

Sociologists who have used Freudian theory have nearly always done so to add to and expand upon an already existing theory of society. In the case of Parsons and those influenced by his approach there was a theory of society based on his systems approach. This led to an over-emphasis on the Freudian contribution to a theory of personality development and the internalization of cultural symbols including the moulding of emotions by cultural symbols. In Freud's own work the notion of unconscious id impulses based on the theory of sexual and death instincts was a fundamental component of his theory. Without this emphasis in a sociology of socialization the Freudian notion of conflicts between these impulses and cultural values is lost. This has become a major flaw in the work of those sociologists who use Freud and psychoanalysis using the Parsonian approach.

Other groups of sociologists and social theorists have had a prior commitment to a Marxist analysis of capitalist societies. This is true of most critical theorists and structuralists. This emphasis upon Marxist sociology and political economy does sensitize these groups of writers to issues concerned with conflict, and makes the Freudian emphasis on conflict easier to assimilate than into Parsonian sociology. However, it tends to mask the possibility of a Freudian analysis of socialist societies and movements in the contemporary world, especially those calling themselves 'Marxist'. The same point can be applied to the Women's Movement and the Gay Movement. All these movements could be analysed from a Freudian perspective using the seminal work of Freud on groups, crowds, authority, and hostility to others. Such an analysis is necessary if these movements are not to become too governed themselves by unconscious feelings and thus fail to reach their goals of a freer society and culture based on reason as far as possible, and not upon force, nor upon irrational adherence to moral values representing the will of the primal father.

Freud's theory of socialization, of gender and sexuality, and of culture and society, has been developed and used by some writers to develop a specific perspective towards these issues which could be called 'Freudian social theory'. Such an approach does not try to link Freudian theory prematurely to other theories of society, whether Marxist or Parsonian, or to a politics of the left or the right. Rather it allows Freudian theory to develop in its own way and in its own area of discourse. This may be expected to be developed further in future. Such a theory will retain the emphasis Freud made on the fundamental notion of unconscious wishes, on the need for a concept of rationality, and on the social and cultural aspects of psychoanalysis.

NOTES AND REFERENCES

[1] S. Freud, *The Question of Lay Analysis* (1926), Standard Edition, Volume 20, Hogarth Press, London. Postscript added 1927.

[2] K. Popper, *Conjectures and Refutations*, Routledge & Kegan Paul, London (1963).

[3] P. Ricoeur, *Freud and Philosophy*, Yale University Press, USA (1970), discusses the hermeneutic view of psychoanalysis alongside the view that it is a causal, explanatory theory too.

[4] T. Parsons, 'The super-ego and the theory of social systems', *Psychiatry*, Vol. 15, pp. 15-25, USA, The William Alanson White Psychiatric Foundation Inc. Reprinted in P. Roazan (editor), *Sigmund Freud*, Prentice-Hall, Englewood Cliffs, N.J. (1973), and in T. Parsons, *Social Structure and Personality*, Free Press, New York (1964). Reference to Roazen, pp. 104-5.

[5] T. Parsons, 'The articulation of the personality and the social action system: Sigmund Freud and Max Weber', Chapter 4 in M. Albin (editor), *New Directions in Psychohistory*, Lexington Books, Lexington, Mass. (1980).

[6] N. Chodorow, *The Reproduction of Mothering: Psychoanalysis and the Sociology of Gender*, University of California Press, Berkeley (1978).

[7] J. Habermas, *Knowledge and Human Interests*, translated by J. Shapiro, Heinemann, London (1972). See especially Chapters 10 and 11.

[8] J. Habermas, 'Sytematically distorted communication' in P. Connerton (editor), *Critical Sociology*, Chapter 17. Penguin, Harmondsworth (1976).

[9] C. Badcock, *The Psychoanalysis of Culture*, Blackwell, Oxford (1980), pp. 232-3.

[10] See for example P. Berger, *Invitation to Sociology*, Penguin, Harmondsworth (1963).

[11] C. Badcock, op cit., see note 9 above, p. 7.

[12] Ibid., p. 36.

[13] R. Jacoby, *Social Amnesia*, Beacon Press, USA (1975), and Harvester Press, Hassocks, Sussex (1977), p. 1.

Suggestions for Further Reading

For students of sociology who are interested in reading Freud the most accessible texts are *The Future of an Illusion* (1927) (S.E. Vol. XXI) and *Civilization and its Discontents* (1930) (S.E. Vol. XXI). The first chapter of the latter text takes up criticisms of the former one. Together the two provide a good overview of Freud's theory of religion and of his critique of modern society.

Those who wish to study Freud in more detail could read *Totem and Taboo* (1913) (S.E. Vol. XIII) and then go on to read the *Introductory Lectures on Psychoanalysis* (1916–17) (S.E. Vols. XV and XVI) and the *New Introductory Lectures on Psychoanalysis* (1933) (S.E. Vol. XXII). (These lectures are published in The Pelican Freud Library as Volumes 1 and 2, and are available in Britain and Australia.) The James Strachey translation is the best to read, and is the one used in The Pelican Freud Library, and in *The Standard Edition of the Complete Psychological Works of Sigmund Freud* (abbreviated to S.E. followed by the volume number here).

Anyone who is especially interested in issues concerning psychoanalysis and women, or psychoanalysis and homosexuality, should read the *Three Essays on the Theory of Sexuality* (1905) (S.E. Vol. VII). The Pelican Freud Library, Volume 7, *On Sexuality* (1977) contains the *Three Essays* and many of Freud's papers which are relevant to the issues concerning psychoanalysis, gender and sexuality.

The developments of Freud's social theory which have been made by later writers and which are of especial interest to sociologists are: Wilhelm Reich, *The Mass Psychology of Fascism* (1970, first published in 1946), and the same author's *The Sexual Revolution* (1972, first published in 1925 and Part II in 1935); this second book is especially concerned with a critique of the changes made in the Soviet Union after 1917, first by Lenin towards sexual liberation, and subsequently reversed by Stalin. Erich Fromm's *The Fear of Freedom* (1942) discusses the history of Germany, from Luther to Hitler, using some of Freud's ideas. Fromm's *The Sane Society* (1955) develops a psychoanalytically informed critique of American society. Some of Fromm's best, and earlier, papers appear in *The Crisis of Psychoanalysis: Essays on Freud, Marx, and Social Psychology* (1970). Herbert Marcuse was critical of Fromm and his criticisms are discussed alongside Fromm's responses in R. Bocock, *Freud and Modern Society* (1976) Chapter 8. Marcuse's most important text on Freud was *Eros and Civilization*, first published in 1955. This should be easier to understand for those who have read Freud's *Civilization and its Discontents*. The work of Jurgen Habermas is discussed by D. Held in *Introduction to Critical Theory* (1980), especially in Part Two. Habermas is also critically discussed in R. Keat's *The Politics of Social Theory: Habermas, Freud, and the Critique of Positivism* (1981). Keat is critical of Habermas for underestimating the importance of the instinct theory in Freud.

Another book which continues in the tradition of critical theory in an interesting and lively way is R. Jacoby's *Social Amnesia: A Critique of Conformist Psychology from Adler to Laing* (1975).

The books which have appeared on the relations between psychoanalysis and women, and psychoanalysis and homosexuality, divide into those which are very critical of Freud, and those which attempt to rescue Freud from the criticisms and to use his ideas in developing an understanding of the position of women and gays. Juliet Mitchell's *Psychoanalysis and Feminism* (1974) opens with difficult sections on Freud's theory of the development of women. Part Two, Section One, critically discusses the work of Reich and Laing, and Part Two, Section Two, critically discusses the work of feminists who have been anti-Freud. This remains the seminal text on the topic from a Freudian point of view.

Guy Hocquenghem's *Homosexual Desire* (1972, French; 1978, English) develops ideas produced by two post-Lacanians G. Deleuze and F. Guattari in their book *Anti-Oedipus* (1972, French; 1977,

English). This is not an easy area to follow because it assumes a great deal of familiarity on the part of the reader with debates in France concerning Lacan's work. Hocquenghem uses a central notion of Lacan, namely desire, and links this with the theme of *Anti-Oedipus* which is that sexual desire is free-floating unless trapped by oedipal family structures.

S. Turkle's *Psychoanalytic Politics; Freud's French Revolution* (1978) provides a readable guide to Lacan and debates surrounding his ideas. Sherry Turkle is a sociologist and so writes from outside the inner world of Lacanian psychoanalysis.

A book by R. Endelman, *Psyche and Society: Explorations in Psychoanalytic Sociology* (1981) discusses recent biological and anthropological work on man, and more importantly for sociologists, develops an empiricist critique of the Women's Movement and the Gay Movement. The book is reasonably well founded in some of Freud's ideas, but there is no serious discussion of the *social* theory of Freud. This is a pity because it does flaw the book.

M. Foucault, *The History of Sexuality, Volume 1, An Introduction* (1978) provides a good analysis of sexuality as an historical construct. Foucault discusses psychoanalysis alongside other discourses which construct and control the erotic lives of children, adolescents, women and perverse adults.

Index

A

Adorno, Theodor, 18, 19, 133, 137
Althusser, Louis, 14, 18, 22
anthropology, 59–60, 82, 136–7
anti-semitism, 22, 27, 110–14
archaic heritage, 62–3, 77, 113–14,
    135
army, 94
art, 80, 105–6, 116
atheism, 101
authority, 94, 97, 114–15, 133

B

Badcock, Christopher, 133–6
Berger, Peter, 134
Beyond the Pleasure Principle, 71–4,
    76
bisexuality, 47, 50, 54–7, 66, 76

C

children, 41–4, 48–50, 58, 82, 87–90,
    103, 113–14, 116
Chodorow, Nancy, 126–8

church, 45, 94
Civilization and its Discontents, 104–9
class, 100, 102, 114, 117–18
clinical practice, 25, 39, 127–37
Comte, Auguste, 87
critical theory, 18, 20, 22, 25, 79,
    123–4, 132–3, 137
crowds, 63, 92–4
cultural superego, 109, 133
culture, 20, 49, 51, 64, 99–100, 105,
    113

D

death instincts, 71–4, 78, 86–7, 95,
    104, 107–8, 126, 131, 133
desire, 36, 42, 66,.84, 109, 115
Dora, 38, 95
Durkheim, Emile, 23, 27, 72–3, 82–3,
    123, 125, 136

E

Ego and the Id, The, 75–8
Electra, 51

Endleman, Robert, 60
Erikson, Erik, 58-9

F

family, 59-60, 106
Feuerbach, Ludwig, 17
Frankfurt school, 14, 18-19, 123
Freud, Sigmund, life and biographical background, 26-9
Fromm, Erich, 19, 25, 127, 133
Future of an Illusion, The, 99-104.

G

gay movement, 21, 24, 55, 63-7, 138
Group Psychology, 92-9
guilt, 78, 108

H

Habermas, Jurgan, 18, 20, 132-3
Hocquenghem, Guy, 23, 66
homosexuality, 38-9, 46, 53, 66, 81, 84, 105

I

incest taboo, 83, 91, 112
instincts, 37, 96, 100, 114, 126
Interpretation of Dreams, The, 33-4, 49, 75

J

Jacoby, Russell, 137
jokes, 35-6
Jones, Ernest, 31n., 130
judaism, 110-14
Judge Schreber, 75
Jung, Carl, 15, 27, 33, 40-1, 51, 54, 58, 65, 95, 129

K

Klein, Melanie, 57, 60-1, 130

L

Lacan, Jacques, 14, 18, 21-5, 35, 58, 66, 124, 128-9

language, 23-4, 35-6, 113
LeBon, Gustav, 92-3
Leonardo da Vinci and a Memory of his Childhood, 80, 105
lesbianism, 46, 81, 84
Lévi-Strauss, Claude, 82, 136
Little Hans, 43, 73, 89, 90

M

Malinowski, Bronislaw, 59-60
Marcuse, Herbert, 14, 18, 25, 63-4, 74, 133
Marx, Karl, and Marxism/Marxists, 17, 19, 23, 25, 28, 39, 72, 79, 96, 99, 113, 115, 117-18, 124, 133
men, 29, 52, 56, 62, 66-7, 126-7
mental illness, 57
methodology, 89, 121-37
Michelangelo, 105
Mitchell, Juliet, 23, 28, 63, 128
morality, 44-9, 80-1, 101, 116
Moses and Monotheism, 22, 29, 98, 109-15

N

narcissism, 75
nazism/fascism, 19, 22, 27-9, 93, 98, 110
negation, 97
neurosis, 46, 80, 84, 86, 112, 115
   war, 71-2
Nietzsche, Fredrich, 17, 79

O

object-relations, 57, 126-7
Oedipus, 34, 48-57, 76, 90
over-determined phenomena, 88

P

Pareto, Vifredo, 17
Parsons, Talcott, 18, 20, 23, 41, 123-8
patriarchy, 28, 67, 90, 111, 128
pleasure principle, 71-4, 104
Popper, Karl, 121-2
property, 107

psychoanalysis,
  organisation, 14–15
  social theory, 15, 70, 128–9, 133–6

R
rationality, 82–3, 98–9, 116–17, 123–5
Reich, Wilhelm, 19, 25, 28, 65, 93, 133
religion, 14, 34, 45, 72–3, 79–92, 100–5, 110–18, 129
repression, 75–7
  surplus, 63–4
return of the repressed, 22, 112–13
revolution, Russian, 28, 55, 98, 117–18
ritual, 85–91, 113, 135

S
Sartre, Jean Paul, 21, 24, 131
science, 87, 103–4
  psychoanalysis as, 18, 25, 35–6, 95, 98, 115–7, 121–5, 129
sexuality, sexual instincts, 37–48, 54, 104–5, 126
slips of the tongue or pen, 34–5
socialization, 18, 36, 41, 44, 47, 57–9
sociology, American, 20, 125–7
  and Freud, 13–16, 120
stigma, 84
structuralism, 18, 82, 124, 128
Studies on Hysteria, 41, 75
sublimation, 45–6, 80
superego, 52, 56, 61, 74–9, 104, 108

symbolic interactionism, 65–6
symbol, 34, 42, 90–1, 113

T
therapy, 37, 42, 55, 58–9, 65, 71–2, 86, 108, 117, 129–32, 134
Three Essays on the Theory of Sexuality, 38–40, 47
Totem and Taboo, 81–93, 97–8

U
unconscious, 23, 32–5, 37, 40, 76, 122, 127–9
  before Freud, 16–18
universities, 132–3
  and psychoanalysis, 14–15, 25

V
Vienna, 26–7, 29, 44, 98, 109
violence, 29, 117, 131

W
war, 72
Weber, Max, 18, 27, 82, 89, 93, 97, 116, 123, 125
Weinstein, Fred,
  (and Platt, Gerald), 126, 128
Winnicott, Donald, 57
women and Women's Movement, 21, 24, 28, 46, 53, 55–7, 60–4, 106, 126–7, 138
Wrong, Dennis, 41